The Iliad: What Homer Reveals About Pride and Leadership Failure

The Human Cost of Ego, Power, and Broken Leadership

Ancient Wisdom Hacks

Published by NX, Inc.

Table of Contents

Preface

Purpose of the Framework
Why *The Iliad* Is Read Here as a Failure Archive, Not a Heroic Epic

PART I: THE REALITY OF HUMAN FAILURE

(Why systems break through people)

Chapter 1: Victory Does Not End Conflict
Outcomes do not resolve resentment
Success intensifies internal fracture
Winning accelerates human cost

Chapter 2: Leaders Are Not Rational Actors Under Injury
Status injury overrides logic
Humiliation outlasts material loss
Pride resists correction

Chapter 3: Ego Is a Strategic Variable
Ego shapes perception of fairness

Ego determines willingness to cooperate
Ignored ego becomes opposition

Chapter 4: Cost Is Paid by People, Not Systems

Systems absorb loss; people internalize it
Moral injury compounds silently
Loyalty erodes before rebellion appears

PART II: THE HUMAN PRIMITIVES

(Irreducible forces that shape collective failure)

Chapter 5: Pride

Pride as identity defense
Pride as resistance to hierarchy
Pride as escalation trigger

Chapter 6: Honor

Honor as social currency
Honor violations outweigh material loss
Private compensation cannot repair public injury

Chapter 7: Status

Status determines voice, not rank
Status loss destabilizes coalitions
Unequal recognition breeds withdrawal

Chapter 8: Loyalty

Loyalty is conditional, not permanent

Loyalty responds to treatment, not rhetoric
Betrayal often begins as silence

Chapter 9: Grief
Loss reshapes priorities
Grief narrows decision horizons
Grieving leaders do not optimize—they react

PART III: COALITION DYNAMICS

(Why alliances collapse internally)

Chapter 10: Coalitions Are Fragile by Default
Multiple incentives coexist uneasily
Alignment requires constant maintenance
Shared enemies do not guarantee unity

Chapter 11: Humiliation as a Breaking Event
Public disrespect fractures alignment
Humiliation invites withdrawal or sabotage
Apologies rarely reverse it

Chapter 12: Unequal Burden, Unequal Cost
Disproportionate sacrifice breeds resentment
Invisible contribution erodes trust
Reward mismatch destabilizes unity

Chapter 13: Withdrawal as Strategic Collapse
Silent disengagement precedes open conflict

Non-participation is a warning signal
Coalitions often die quietly

PART IV: FAILURE MODES OF LEADERSHIP

(How leaders accelerate collapse unintentionally)

Chapter 14: Public Assertion of Authority
Public dominance invites resistance
Authority asserted loudly is already weakening
Force replaces legitimacy when pride is injured

Chapter 15: Emotional Decision Contagion
Leader emotion spreads through systems
Rage, fear, and grief propagate
Discipline collapses without visible restraint

Chapter 16: Misreading Silence
Silence interpreted as agreement
Silence often signals injury
Silence precedes fracture

Chapter 17: Moral Injury
Violating personal or collective codes
Injury persists even after victory
Moral cost compounds long-term damage

PART V: APPLICATION WITHOUT REPAIR

(Why this framework diagnoses but does not solve)

Chapter 18: Leadership in Organizations
Performance without recognition
Public correction vs. private dignity
Why high performers disengage

Chapter 19: Political and Institutional Coalitions
Factional pride
Status competition
Legitimacy collapse through disrespect

Chapter 20: Crisis, Loss, and Aftermath
Trauma reshapes leadership behavior
Grief overrides procedural logic
Systems fail quietly after visible success

PART VI: RELATION TO OTHER FRAMEWORKS

(Why this framework is necessary but insufficient alone)

Chapter 21: Why *The Art of War* Is Insufficient
Correct decisions can still destroy morale
Cost models ignore emotional injury
Restraint does not heal humiliation

Chapter 22: Why *The Prince* Is Insufficient
Power can persist while coalitions rot
Authority cannot command loyalty
Legitimacy does not repair pride

FINAL POSITIONING

What the Iliad Framework Is—and Is Not
A failure-diagnostic system
A human-cost lens
A coalition-fracture model

Not a leadership guide
Not a reconciliation manual
Not a hero's journey

Used correctly, it does not make leadership easier.
It makes failure visible before it is irreversible.

End Matter

Before You Close This Book
A Final Warning About Quiet Collapse

PREFACE

The Purpose of the Framework

This book does not treat *The Iliad* as literature.
It does not treat it as myth.
It does not treat it as a guide to virtue, leadership, or heroism.

This book treats *The Iliad* as a **failure record**.

A structured archive of how intelligent leaders, dominant warriors, rational coalitions, and technically superior systems **collapse from the inside**—not because strategy failed, but because *people did*.

That distinction matters.

Modern readers are trained—almost conditioned—to read *The Iliad* as a story of greatness: of honor, courage, sacrifice, rage, and fate. They are taught to admire Achilles, respect Hector, pity Priam, and mourn the tragedy of war. Entire academic disciplines orbit questions of morality, destiny, masculinity, and virtue within the poem.

This framework rejects all of that.

Not because those interpretations are wrong—but because they are **operationally useless**.

The modern world does not fail because people lack stories about honor.

It fails because leaders, systems, and coalitions **misdiagnose the source of collapse**.

They assume failure comes from:

- Poor planning

- Insufficient power

- External opposition

- Bad intelligence

- Moral weakness

The Iliad demonstrates—repeatedly, relentlessly—that collapse more often comes from something far less visible and far more dangerous:

Human response under pressure.

This framework exists to formalize that reality.

The Core Question This Framework Answers

This book is organized around a single diagnostic question:

Why do leaders, coalitions, and systems collapse even when strategy is sound and power is intact?

That question is not theoretical. It is not literary. It is not philosophical.

It is practical.

History is full of systems that *should* have held:

- Armies with numerical superiority

- Coalitions with shared interests

- Leaders with legitimate authority

- Institutions with entrenched power

- Organizations with proven strategy

Yet they fracture anyway.

They fracture despite planning.
 They fracture despite advantage.
 They fracture despite intelligence.
 They fracture despite precedent.

The Iliad is not an anomaly in this regard—it is the **clearest early record** of the pattern.

The Greeks have:

- Superior fighters

- Superior tactics

- A unified enemy

- A shared objective

- Time on their side

And yet the war stalls, decays, and metastasizes into internal conflict.

Not because Troy is invincible.

But because the Greek system becomes **psychologically ungovernable**.

This framework treats that failure not as tragedy—but as data.

Reframing *The Iliad*: From Epic to Diagnostic System

The Iliad opens not with victory, wisdom, or destiny—but with a malfunction:

> *"Sing, goddess, the rage of Achilles…"*

Rage—not strategy, not justice, not fate—is the initiating condition.

From the first line, the poem signals that what follows is not a story of warcraft, but a study in **emotional ignition and systemic fallout**.

The framework formalized in this book rests on a simple premise:

> *The Iliad is not about how wars are won.*
> *It is about how wars are lost when humans break alignment.*

In AWH terms, *The Iliad* functions as a **failure-diagnostic framework** with four recurring layers:

1. **Individual emotional rupture**

2. **Leader ego collision**

3. **Coalition fracture**

4. **Cost displacement onto non-decision-makers**

Each layer compounds the next.

Each failure is rationalized.
Each escalation is justified.
Each cost is deferred—until it is paid in blood, exile, or irreversible loss.

This framework makes those layers explicit.

What This Framework Does

1. It Diagnoses Human Failure Modes

Most strategic frameworks assume rational actors.

The Iliad does not.

It assumes:

- Pride

- Status sensitivity

- Humiliation response

- Identity threat

- Withdrawal as protest

- Overreaction as compensation

Achilles is not irrational in a clinical sense. He is *emotionally consistent*.

Agamemnon is not incompetent. He is *status-protective.*

The failure is not madness—it is **misalignment between emotional reality and strategic necessity**.

This framework identifies recurring failure modes such as:

- Ego over-indexing on symbolic loss

- Status injury treated as existential threat

- Withdrawal framed as moral protest

- Punishment of the group to discipline the leader

- Escalation driven by humiliation rather than advantage

These are not ancient problems.

They are executive problems.
Founder problems.
Coalition problems.
Institutional problems.

The framework names them so they can be **recognized before they metastasize**.

---

2. It Explains Coalition Fracture

The Greek coalition does not collapse because its members disagree on the objective.

They collapse because **alignment is psychological before it is strategic**.

Achilles and Agamemnon want the same outcome.
They even understand the same risks.

What they do not share is **status hierarchy agreement**.

Once that fractures, the coalition becomes brittle.

This framework tracks:

- How personal disputes contaminate group incentives

- How silence becomes sabotage

- How withdrawal masquerades as principle

- How leaders misread noncompliance as disloyalty rather than injury

The Iliad shows that coalitions fail *quietly first.*

Not with open rebellion—but with disengagement.

---

3. It Exposes Ego, Pride, and Humiliation as Strategic Forces

Traditional strategy treats ego as noise.

This framework treats ego as **terrain**.

Achilles does not withdraw because the war is unjust.
He withdraws because his *identity* has been violated.

Agamemnon does not provoke Achilles because he is stupid.
He provokes him because conceding status feels more
dangerous than losing men.

The Iliad repeatedly demonstrates a rule this framework
formalizes:

> **Humiliation reshapes decision-making faster than
> logic.**

Once humiliation enters the system:

- Strategy becomes secondary

- Outcomes become symbolic

- Loss is acceptable if dignity is preserved

This framework does not moralize that behavior.
It **maps it**.

---

4. It Tracks Cost Paid by People Rather Than Systems

Systems rarely pay for their own failure.

People do.

The Greek command structure remains intact.
The war continues.
The leaders persist.

Meanwhile:

- Soldiers die in Achilles' absence

- Allies bear losses for private disputes

- Non-decision-makers absorb the cost

The framework insists on tracking *who pays* for dysfunction.

Because systems that do not internalize cost **repeat failure**.

---

5. It Reveals Why Rational Frameworks Fail in Emotional Environments

Every rational argument in *The Iliad* fails.

Not because it is wrong—but because it arrives **after emotional commitment** has already locked behavior.

This framework identifies the critical error:

> *Reason applied too late does not persuade—it irritates.*

Once pride is engaged, logic is interpreted as insult.

The framework therefore treats timing, emotional state, and identity threat as **preconditions for strategy**, not footnotes.

What This Framework Does Not Do

This book is explicit about its limits.

It Does Not Glorify Heroism

Heroism is not a solution in this framework—it is often a **symptom of systemic failure**.

Achilles' greatness does not save the Greeks.
 It nearly destroys them.

Hero narratives obscure failure patterns by personalizing outcomes.

This framework removes the halo.

It Does Not Provide Leadership Advice

There are no "do this instead" prescriptions here.

Because advice presumes:

- Control

- Receptivity

- Moral clarity

The Iliad demonstrates that leaders often possess none of these when it matters.

This framework is diagnostic, not instructional.

It Does Not Offer Reconciliation Tactics

Reconciliation assumes willingness.

Achilles is unwilling.
 Agamemnon is defensive.
 The system moves forward regardless.

This framework studies breakdown **without assuming repair**.

It Does Not Resolve Moral Injury

The Iliad is full of moral injury.
 This framework does not heal it.

It identifies how moral injury:

- Hardens positions

- Freezes decision-making

- Justifies withdrawal

Resolution is outside scope.

It Is Designed to Identify Where Strategy and Power Are Undone by Human Response

That is the point.

Not to inspire.
 Not to console.
 Not to elevate.

But to **see clearly**.

Why This Framework Exists Now

Modern systems are increasingly:

- Interdependent

- Psychologically fragile

- Status-sensitive

- Publicly performative

The same failure patterns visible in *The Iliad* now play out in:

- Corporate collapses

- Political coalitions

- Startup implosions

- Social movements

- Military engagements

- Cultural institutions

Power remains.
Strategy remains.
Alignment breaks anyway.

This framework exists to answer *why*—without comforting myths.

How to Read This Book

Do not read it as history.
Do not read it as philosophy.
Do not read it as self-help.

Read it as:

- A diagnostic manual

- A failure archive

- A system stress test

Each chapter isolates a failure mechanism.
 Each section maps consequence.
 Each conclusion resists moralization.

The goal is not to become heroic.

The goal is to become **precise**.

Final Positioning

This framework repositions *The Iliad* as:

- A failure-diagnostic engine

- A coalition fracture map

- A human cost ledger

- A warning against emotional blindness

It is not:

- A leadership philosophy

- A moral system

- A redemption story

Used correctly, it does not make you bold.

It makes you accurate.

And in environments where power is intact but collapse is imminent, accuracy is the only advantage that matters.

PART I

THE REALITY OF HUMAN FAILURE

Why Systems Break Through People

Chapter 1

Victory Does Not End Conflict

Core Insight

Conflict persists after decisions are settled.

---

1. The False Assumption at the Center of Strategy

Most systems—military, political, corporate, institutional—are built on a quiet but catastrophic assumption:

That outcomes resolve conflict.

This assumption is rarely stated explicitly. It does not need to be. It is embedded in how strategies are designed, how wars are planned, how negotiations are concluded, and how leaders speak once a decision has been made.

Victory is expected to close the loop.
A decision is expected to restore order.
A win is expected to unify.

And when it does not, the system responds with confusion rather than diagnosis.

The problem is not that victory sometimes fails.

The problem is that **victory was never designed to address the real source of conflict**.

The Iliad exposes this flaw with brutal clarity.

The war is already decided long before the poem ends. Troy's fate is sealed. The Greeks possess superior force, superior champions, and overwhelming momentum. Even the gods understand the outcome.

And yet conflict does not contract—it **multiplies**.

Why?

Because outcomes resolve objectives.
They do not resolve **resentment**.

This chapter formalizes a core AWH principle:

> **Victory ends contests. It does not end human opposition.**

2. The Difference Between Resolution and Termination

Strategy confuses two fundamentally different concepts:

- **Resolution**: an outcome is achieved

- **Termination**: conflict ceases

Systems are excellent at resolution.
They are poor at termination.

Resolution is structural.
Termination is psychological.

The Greeks resolve the strategic problem of Troy.
They never terminate the emotional war within their own ranks.

The Iliad opens after years of fighting. The objective is unchanged. The enemy is contained. The siege is functional. The system should be stabilizing.

Instead, it destabilizes from within.

The poem does not begin with Trojan brilliance or Greek failure.

It begins with **internal rupture**.

> *"Sing, goddess, the rage of Achilles, son of Peleus,*
> *that caused the Greeks untold pain…"*

The war does not escalate because Troy adapts.

It escalates because the Greek system **cannot metabolize success without fracture**.

This is not incidental. It is diagnostic.

---

3. Why Winning Intensifies Internal Fracture

Victory increases pressure on identity.

Before success, failure can be externalized.
 After success, blame turns inward.

Once a system is winning, three destabilizing dynamics accelerate:

1. **Status sensitivity increases**

2. **Symbolic losses become intolerable**

3. **Internal hierarchy disputes replace external threat**

The Iliad captures this precisely.

Agamemnon is not losing the war when he seizes Briseis.

He is asserting dominance **during advantage**.

Achilles is not endangering the Greeks because the war is unwinnable.

He withdraws **because winning without dignity feels like defeat**.

This is the paradox victory introduces:

> **When survival is no longer at stake, identity becomes the battlefield.**

The system does not fail under pressure.
It fails under *relief*.

---

4. Outcomes Do Not Resolve Resentment

Resentment is not logical.
It is relational.

It does not dissipate when a goal is achieved.
It intensifies when a grievance is left unacknowledged.

Achilles' grievance is not strategic.
It is symbolic.

Briseis is not valuable as an asset.
She is valuable as recognition.

Agamemnon's decision does not weaken the army materially.

It fractures it **psychologically**.

And once resentment enters the system, outcomes lose their pacifying power.

The Greeks continue to fight.
 They continue to win battles.
 They continue to press Troy.

But resentment now operates as a parallel force—undermining cohesion without ever confronting the enemy.

This is the AWH diagnostic:

> **Resentment survives success.**
> **It feeds on it.**

---

5. Victory Narrows Moral Bandwidth

Another hidden effect of winning is **moral compression**.

When survival is uncertain, leaders tolerate dissent.
 When victory appears inevitable, dissent feels like betrayal.

Agamemnon cannot afford to appear weak—not because Troy threatens him, but because his authority is now visible.

Achilles cannot tolerate humiliation—not because it changes the war, but because it redefines his place within it.

Victory removes ambiguity.
 Ambiguity is where compromise lives.

Once ambiguity collapses, every dispute becomes existential.

This is why *The Iliad* grows more violent, not less, as the war progresses.

Not because the enemy strengthens.

But because the **human cost is no longer absorbed by uncertainty**.

---

6. Winning Accelerates Human Cost

One of the most dangerous myths in strategy is that success reduces cost.

In reality, success often **front-loads** it.

The longer Achilles stays withdrawn, the more Greek soldiers die.

The system continues to function.
 The command structure remains intact.
 The war effort persists.

But the cost is redistributed downward.

This is a recurring AWH pattern:

> **Systems protect themselves by displacing cost onto people.**

Victory enables this displacement because it masks internal failure.

As long as Troy still stands, losses can be justified.
 As long as the war continues, suffering can be rationalized.

Achilles' absence becomes a background condition rather than a crisis—until it cannot be ignored.

The system tolerates dysfunction **because the outcome still seems achievable**.

---

7. Conflict After Decision: The Post-Outcome Zone

Most frameworks end their analysis at the decision point.

The Iliad begins there.

The poem is not interested in *whether* Troy will fall.

It is interested in what happens **after the answer is already known**.

This is the post-outcome zone:

- The phase after strategy

- The phase after commitment

- The phase after consensus

It is where most modern failures occur.

Mergers collapse after contracts are signed.
Coalitions fracture after elections are won.
Organizations implode after targets are met.

Because the decision resolved the objective—but activated unresolved human responses.

This framework insists on examining that zone.

---

8. Why Systems Cannot Self-Correct After Victory

Failure before victory triggers reform.

Failure after victory triggers denial.

This is because success creates narrative insulation.

As long as progress continues, leaders interpret dissent as noise.

Achilles is dismissed.
 Warnings are ignored.
 Losses are reframed as acceptable.

The system does not course-correct because it does not perceive itself as failing.

This is the most dangerous phase of any system's lifecycle.

> **The moment when it is still working—but already broken.**

---

9. The Illusion of Closure

Modern systems crave closure.

They celebrate:

- Endings

- Conclusions

- Final decisions

- Signed agreements

The Iliad offers none.

Even Hector's death does not close the war.
Even Patroclus' funeral does not restore alignment.
Even Achilles' return does not heal the system.

Each "resolution" opens new wounds.

The poem refuses closure because closure is a lie systems tell themselves.

Conflict ends when people disengage emotionally—not when outcomes are achieved.

---

10. Strategic Implication (Without Prescription)

This framework does not offer advice.

It offers diagnosis.

If victory does not end conflict, then:

- Outcomes cannot be relied on for stability

- Success cannot be assumed to unify

- Decisions cannot be treated as final

And any system that treats winning as an endpoint is structurally blind.

The Iliad does not warn us about enemies.

It warns us about **ourselves after success**.

---

11. The First Failure Pattern Established

This chapter establishes the first recurring failure pattern that will echo throughout the framework:

> **Conflict persists after decisions are settled**
> **because humans do not experience closure the**
> **way systems do.**

Systems end processes.
 Humans carry memory.

Until that gap is acknowledged, every victory plants the seeds of the next fracture.

Closing Position

The Iliad is not a story about how wars are fought.

It is a record of what happens **after winning begins**.

Victory does not end conflict.
 It relocates it.

From the battlefield
 to the hierarchy
 to the ego
 to the people who pay the cost

This framework begins here because every failure that follows depends on this truth.

If you believe winning ends conflict, you will never see collapse coming.

And by the time you do, the decision will already be settled—
 and the damage irreversible.

Chapter 2

Leaders Are Not Rational Actors Under Injury

Failure Mode

Assuming leaders behave rationally after disrespect.

---

1. The Most Dangerous Assumption in Strategy

Nearly every strategic framework—ancient or modern—rests on an implicit belief:

> **That leaders, once informed, will act in their own best interest.**

This belief survives despite overwhelming evidence to the contrary.

It survives boardroom implosions.
It survives political self-sabotage.
It survives military catastrophes.

And it survives *The Iliad*—even though the poem dismantles it line by line.

Leaders are rational **until** they are injured.

After injury, they remain intelligent, capable, and decisive—but no longer aligned with outcome optimization. Their behavior reorganizes around a different objective:

Restoring threatened identity.

This chapter formalizes a core AWH principle:

Status injury overrides logic faster than fear overrides courage.

Once injured, a leader's decision-making environment changes. Inputs that once mattered lose relevance. Advice becomes provocation. Evidence becomes insult. Delay becomes defiance.

The failure is not ignorance.

It is **reorientation**.

---

2. What Counts as Injury in Leadership Systems

In *The Iliad*, injury is rarely physical.

It is symbolic.

Agamemnon is not wounded in battle when Achilles confronts him. Achilles is not impoverished when Briseis is taken.

The injury is **status displacement**.

Briseis is not valuable as property.
She is valuable as *recognition*.

Agamemnon's seizure is not a logistical act.
It is a public declaration of hierarchy.

Achilles' response is not emotional excess.
It is identity defense.

This framework defines **status injury** as:

- Public diminishment

- Loss of symbolic recognition

- Undermining of rank or role

- Exposure of vulnerability

- Forced submission without consent

These injuries do not fade with explanation.
They do not heal with compensation.
They do not dissolve when the system moves forward.

They **persist**.

---

3. Why Rationality Collapses After Disrespect

Rational models assume stable priorities.

Status injury destabilizes priority structure.

Once injured, a leader's hierarchy of concerns reorders as follows:

1. Identity preservation

2. Status restoration

3. Narrative control

4. Only then—outcomes

This is not pathology.
It is human.

Achilles does not miscalculate the cost of withdrawal.

He accepts it.

He knows Greek soldiers will die.
He knows the war will stall.
He knows Troy benefits.

And he chooses it anyway.

Why?

Because humiliation **outlasts material loss**.

This is the first irreversible break from rational-actor theory.

> **When dignity is threatened, loss becomes tolerable.**

4. The Error of Post-Injury Logic

One of the most common failures in leadership systems is timing.

Logic is introduced **after** injury.

Counselors appeal to reason.
 Allies invoke shared goals.
 Subordinates point to consequences.

In *The Iliad*, this happens repeatedly.

Odysseus argues pragmatically.
 Phoenix appeals emotionally.
 Ajax speaks bluntly.

All fail.

Not because they are wrong.
 But because they are late.

The framework formalizes this rule:

> **Logic applied after humiliation does not persuade—it antagonizes.**

Why?

Because advice assumes cooperation.
 Injury dissolves it.

What the injured leader hears is not guidance—but dominance.

5. Pride Does Not Resist Correction—It Redefines It

Pride is often misunderstood as stubbornness.

In reality, pride is **a filtering mechanism**.

It determines which inputs are admissible.

After injury:

- Agreement feels like surrender

- Compromise feels like erasure

- Concession feels like confirmation of weakness

Achilles does not refuse Agamemnon's gifts because they are insufficient.

He refuses them because accepting them would redefine the injury as justified.

> *"I hate him like the very gates of Hades,*
> *who says one thing but hides another in his heart."*

The gifts solve a material problem.
They do nothing for the symbolic wound.

This is a critical AWH diagnostic:

You cannot compensate symbolic loss with material gain.

---

6. Humiliation Has a Longer Half-Life Than Loss

Material loss can be recovered.
 Status loss lingers.

This is why leaders will sacrifice:

- Revenue

- Territory

- Personnel

- Opportunity

to avoid humiliation.

Achilles sacrifices honor in battle to preserve honor in hierarchy.

Agamemnon sacrifices cohesion to preserve supremacy.

Neither behaves irrationally by their own internal metric.

They are optimizing for **self-definition**, not victory.

This is why humiliation is more destabilizing than defeat.

Defeat ends.
 Humiliation echoes.

---

7. Injury Makes Leaders Dangerous to Their Own Systems

An injured leader is not inert.

They are **active destabilizers**.

Achilles does not defect to Troy.
 He does not sabotage supply lines.
 He does not rebel openly.

He withdraws.

Withdrawal is the most systemically dangerous form of protest
because it preserves legitimacy while inflicting cost.

The system cannot punish it without escalating fracture.
 It cannot ignore it without bleeding.

This pattern repeats across history and institutions.

The injured leader becomes a **silent veto**.

---

8. Why Correction Fails After Injury

Most systems attempt correction through:

- Incentives

- Appeals to reason

- Moral framing

- Threats

All fail in *The Iliad*.

Why?

Because correction presumes the leader still shares the system's objective.

Injury breaks that assumption.

Once injured, the leader's objective becomes **self-coherence**.

Until that is restored—or rendered irrelevant—correction is impossible.

---

9. The Illusion of Apology as Repair

Agamemnon apologizes.

He admits fault.
He offers compensation.
He acknowledges excess.

And it changes nothing.

Why?

Because apology without status recalibration is procedural, not relational.

The framework identifies this pattern clearly:

> **Apologies that preserve hierarchy do not heal hierarchy injuries.**

Agamemnon remains king.
Achilles remains diminished.

The system expects closure.
The human does not experience it.

---

10. The Cost of Misreading Injured Leaders

The Greeks misread Achilles repeatedly.

They interpret his withdrawal as temporary.
They assume incentives will work.
They expect loyalty to override injury.

Each assumption compounds loss.

This is the central failure mode of this chapter:

> **Assuming leaders behave rationally after disrespect.**

They do not.

They behave *consistently with injury*.

Systems that ignore this reality do not just fail to persuade—they accelerate collapse.

---

11. Modern Echoes of the Same Failure

This is not an ancient pathology.

It appears wherever:

- Founders are sidelined after success

- Executives are publicly undermined

- Political leaders are humiliated by allies

- Military commanders are stripped of symbolic authority

In every case, rational incentives are offered.
In every case, resentment outlasts logic.
In every case, systems are surprised by resistance that was **entirely predictable**.

---

12. Strategic Implication (Without Prescription)

This framework does not advise appeasement.
It does not recommend ego management.
It does not offer reconciliation strategies.

It offers diagnosis.

If leaders are not rational actors under injury, then:

- Post-decision persuasion is unreliable

- Incentives are not neutral

- Authority does not guarantee compliance

- Respect is not ornamental—it is structural

Ignoring this is not realism.
It is blindness.

Closing Position

The Iliad does not depict irrational leaders.

It depicts **injured ones**.

Their decisions are not chaotic.
They are aligned—to a different objective.

Victory does not heal them.
Logic does not reach them.
Correction does not move them.

Until systems learn to recognize this shift, they will continue to mistake pride for madness, resentment for disloyalty, and withdrawal for irrationality.

And they will continue to pay for that mistake in people, not outcomes.

Leaders do not stop being rational under injury.
They stop being rational *for you*.

That is the reality this framework insists we confront.

Chapter 3

Ego Is a Strategic Variable

Principle

Ignored ego becomes opposition.

---

1. The Strategic Blind Spot That Breaks Systems

Most systems pretend ego is irrelevant.

They speak as if ego were:

- A personality quirk

- A leadership flaw

- A maturity issue

- A private weakness

In strategic language, ego is treated as noise—something to be minimized, disciplined, or excluded from serious analysis.

The Iliad demolishes that assumption.

Ego is not noise.
Ego is **signal**.

It shapes how fairness is perceived, how cooperation is granted or withdrawn, and how power is interpreted at the human level.
When ego is dismissed, it does not disappear—it reorganizes into resistance.

This chapter formalizes a core AWH reality:

> **Ego is not opposed to strategy.**
> **Ego is one of its operating conditions.**

Systems that fail to account for ego do not become rational.
They become fragile.

---

2. What Ego Actually Is (and Is Not)

Ego is commonly misunderstood as arrogance.

In reality, ego is **identity integrity**—the internal mechanism that answers three questions:

1. *Who am I within this system?*

2. *How am I recognized?*

3. *What does my position mean relative to others?*

Ego is not vanity.
It is **orientation**.

In *The Iliad*, Achilles' ego is not expressed through boasting or excess pride. It is expressed through **refusal**.

He refuses to fight.
He refuses compensation.
He refuses reconciliation on terms that preserve his diminished status.

Why?

Because ego does not respond to outcomes.
It responds to **recognition**.

---

3. Ego Shapes Perception of Fairness

Fairness is not objective.

It is perceived through ego.

Two actors can receive the same outcome and experience it differently depending on what that outcome communicates about their standing.

Briseis is not Achilles' grievance because she is lost.

She is his grievance because *how* she is taken redefines his place in the hierarchy.

Agamemnon frames the seizure as administrative necessity.
Achilles experiences it as symbolic erasure.

This gap is critical.

The system believes it has acted fairly.
The individual experiences injustice.

This is the AWH diagnostic:

**Fairness is not measured by distribution.
It is measured by meaning.**

Ego is the interpreter.

---

4. Ego Determines Willingness to Cooperate

Cooperation is not compelled by logic.

It is granted by ego.

Achilles does not stop believing the Greeks deserve to win.
He does not dispute the legitimacy of the war.
He does not defect to Troy.

He simply withholds cooperation.

This is the most destabilizing move available to someone with leverage.

Ego decides:

- Whether effort is given freely

- Whether compliance is enthusiastic or minimal

- Whether loyalty is active or symbolic

Systems that rely on authority alone misinterpret compliance as cooperation.

The Iliad shows the difference.

The Greek army still exists.
The chain of command still functions.
But its most powerful asset is disengaged.

The system remains intact.
Its effectiveness collapses.

---

5. Why Ego Responds to Recognition, Not Outcomes

Outcomes are abstract.
Recognition is personal.

A system can deliver success and still alienate its most critical contributors if recognition is mishandled.

Agamemnon offers Achilles wealth, honor, and future glory.

All are rejected.

Why?

Because none alter the **meaning** of the original injury.

Recognition is not transactional.
 It is positional.

This is why ego cannot be managed with incentives alone.

> **You cannot buy back dignity with rewards that assume it was never lost.**

---

6. The Mistake of Treating Ego as Immaturity

One of the most common rationalizations in failing systems is contempt.

Leaders dismiss ego-driven resistance as:

- Childish

- Emotional

- Unprofessional

- Irrational

This dismissal compounds the problem.

Ego does not require validation.
It requires **acknowledgment**.

By reducing ego to immaturity, systems justify ignoring it—and in doing so, convert latent tension into active opposition.

Achilles is not immature.
He is consistent.

He accepts loss.
He accepts death.
He accepts isolation.

What he will not accept is **invisibility**.

---

7. Ego as a Predictive Variable

Because ego follows patterns, it is predictable.

When ego is:

- Recognized → cooperation increases

- Undermined → resistance forms

- Ignored → opposition hardens

This is not psychology.
It is system dynamics.

The Iliad provides repeated confirmation.

Each time Achilles' status is disregarded, the cost escalates.
Each attempt to bypass ego worsens the fracture.

The framework insists on treating ego the way strategy treats terrain:

You may dislike it.
You may wish it away.
But if you ignore it, it will decide the outcome for you.

---

8. How Ignored Ego Becomes Opposition

Ignored ego does not announce itself.

It does not revolt immediately.
It does not always argue.
It often withdraws.

Withdrawal is opposition without confrontation.

Achilles' withdrawal:

- Preserves legitimacy

- Avoids open rebellion

- Maximizes pressure on the system

This is why ignored ego is more dangerous than challenged ego.

Once ego transitions from wounded to oppositional, it begins optimizing for **system discomfort**, not resolution.

The system misreads this as stubbornness.
In reality, it is strategy—just not the system's strategy.

---

9. Ego and the Redistribution of Cost

When ego-driven opposition emerges, systems rarely absorb the cost.

They displace it.

Greek soldiers die.
Allies suffer.
Time is lost.

Meanwhile:

- Agamemnon retains authority

- Achilles retains autonomy

- The system preserves hierarchy

This pattern repeats across institutions.

Ego conflicts are rarely paid for by the people who create them.

They are paid for by those without voice, leverage, or symbolic standing.

This is why ego is not a "soft" issue.
It is a cost allocator.

---

10. Why Systems Keep Making This Mistake

If ego is so clearly consequential, why is it consistently ignored?

Because acknowledging ego requires admitting:

- That authority is not sufficient

- That hierarchy is psychologically fragile

- That systems depend on voluntary alignment

These admissions threaten institutional self-image.

It is easier to pretend ego is irrelevant than to redesign systems that account for it.

The Iliad exposes the cost of that avoidance.

---

11. Modern Systems, Same Variable

This failure pattern is not confined to ancient war.

It appears in:

- Corporate leadership disputes

- Political coalitions

- Creative partnerships

- Military command structures

- Social movements

Everywhere ego is treated as an inconvenience rather than a variable, alignment deteriorates.

The language changes.
 The outcome does not.

---

12. Strategic Implication (Without Prescription)

This framework does not instruct leaders to flatter.
 It does not suggest ego appeasement.
 It does not recommend emotional management.

It provides diagnosis.

If ego is a strategic variable, then:

- Planning without it is incomplete

- Outcomes cannot substitute for recognition

- Authority cannot replace alignment

- Ignored contributors will eventually resist

This is not moral.
 It is mechanical.

Closing Position

The Iliad is not driven by fate.
 It is not driven by gods.
 It is not driven by destiny.

It is driven by **ego mismanaged at scale**.

Achilles does not destroy the Greek war effort by attacking it.

He destroys it by **withholding himself**.

That is the power of ego when ignored.

> **Strategy that dismisses ego does not become rational.**
> **It becomes blind.**

And blind systems do not fail quietly.

They fail through people—
 long after the outcome was supposedly decided.

Chapter 4

Cost Is Paid by People, Not Systems

Core Reality

Systems absorb loss.
 People internalize it.

---

1. The Fundamental Accounting Error in All Systems

Every system tells itself the same lie:

> **That it bears the cost of its own decisions.**

It does not.

Systems are designed to endure.
 People are designed to feel.

That difference is not incidental—it is structural.

When a system fails, it does not bleed.
 When a strategy miscalculates, it does not grieve.
 When leadership fractures, it does not carry shame.

People do.

This chapter formalizes a principle that *The Iliad* demonstrates
with brutal consistency:

> **Systems remain intact by transferring pain to
> individuals who cannot refuse it.**

The Greek war effort does not collapse when Achilles withdraws.

It continues.

The command structure remains.
 The hierarchy remains.
 The objective remains.

But the cost of dysfunction is quietly shifted onto those with the
least agency.

---

2. How Systems "Absorb" Loss

From the outside, the Greek system appears resilient.

Losses are recorded.
 Battles are fought.
 Replacements are made.
 Funerals occur.

The system persists.

This creates the illusion that the system is absorbing damage.

In reality, what is happening is **diffusion**.

Loss is spread thinly enough across individuals that no single failure triggers systemic alarm.

This is the AWH diagnostic:

> **Systems do not feel cumulative loss.**
> **People do.**

Each death matters to someone.
Each humiliation lands somewhere.
Each moral compromise leaves residue.

The system logs numbers.
Humans carry memory.

---

3. The Silent Accumulation of Moral Injury

Moral injury is not trauma in the conventional sense.

It is not fear.
It is not shock.
It is not panic.

It is the internal conflict that arises when individuals are required
to:

- Participate in injustice

- Endure preventable loss

- Obey decisions that violate internal standards

- Watch leaders protect status at the expense of others

In *The Iliad*, moral injury accumulates quietly.

Greek soldiers die not because Troy overwhelms them—but
because Achilles is absent.

They know why he is absent.
 They know the dispute.
 They know it is personal.

And they die anyway.

This is the most corrosive form of injury:

> **To suffer for reasons you know are
> avoidable—and powerless to stop.**

The system does not register this as failure.

But loyalty does.

4. Why Moral Injury Compounds Silently

Moral injury rarely produces immediate rebellion.

It produces compliance.

People continue to fight.
 They follow orders.
 They suppress resentment.

Because rebellion is costly.
 Because dissent is dangerous.
 Because systems punish disruption more reliably than they prevent harm.

So the injury compounds.

Each additional loss confirms a pattern:

- That leadership disputes matter more than lives

- That hierarchy is insulated from consequence

- That sacrifice is expected downward, never upward

This is why moral injury is so dangerous.

It does not announce itself.
 It waits.

5. The Mistake of Measuring Loyalty by Obedience

Systems routinely confuse obedience with loyalty.

They are not the same.

Obedience is enforced.
 Loyalty is voluntary.

In *The Iliad*, Greek soldiers obey orders long after loyalty has begun to erode.

They fight without Achilles.
 They accept losses.
 They endure.

But something has already changed.

They no longer believe the system protects them.
 They no longer believe sacrifice is reciprocal.
 They no longer believe leadership bears cost alongside them.

This is the AWH warning:

When loyalty erodes, obedience becomes brittle.

The system cannot see this erosion because it does not show up in metrics.

Until it does.

---

6. Why Systems Miss the Point of Failure

Systems are designed to detect overt threats:

- Mutiny

- Defection

- Sabotage

- Open dissent

Moral injury produces none of these—at first.

It produces:

- Emotional withdrawal

- Reduced initiative

- Silent compliance

- Cynicism

- Loss of identification with mission

By the time rebellion appears, the system is already hollow.

The Iliad captures this perfectly.

The Greek army does not rebel against Agamemnon.
It simply **fails more often**.

Battles become bloodier.
Confidence erodes.
Heroes die unnecessarily.

The system interprets this as misfortune.

It is not.

It is delayed consequence.

---

7. Cost Displacement as a Survival Mechanism

It is important to be precise here.

Systems do not displace cost accidentally.

They do it **to survive**.

If leaders internalized every loss, no system would function.
If hierarchy collapsed under moral weight, coordination would
cease.

Cost displacement is not evil.
It is structural.

But it has limits.

When too much cost is displaced downward, the system loses the very people it depends on—not through defection, but through disengagement.

Achilles' withdrawal is only the most visible example.

The quieter collapse happens among unnamed soldiers whose deaths are recorded but not remembered.

---

8. The Role of Leaders in Cost Asymmetry

Leadership magnifies cost asymmetry.

Leaders make decisions.
Others pay for them.

This is not inherently unjust.
It is unavoidable.

What becomes destructive is **lack of reciprocity**.

In *The Iliad*, Agamemnon's authority is never personally endangered by the losses he causes.

Achilles' authority is wounded symbolically—but not materially.

Greek soldiers absorb the full physical cost.

This asymmetry becomes intolerable when it is perceived as:

- Unnecessary

- Arbitrary

- Ego-driven

At that point, moral injury accelerates.

---

9. Loyalty Erodes Before Rebellion Appears

This is the most important warning in this chapter.

Rebellion is not the first sign of collapse.

It is the last.

Before rebellion, there is:

- Detachment

- Resignation

- Quiet resentment

- Emotional exit

People stop believing the system deserves them.

They still show up.
 They still perform.
 They still comply.

But the bond is broken.

The Iliad shows this erosion through atmosphere rather than declaration.

The war grows darker.
 Deaths become heavier.
 Honor feels hollow.

The system still functions.

But it no longer inspires.

---

10. Why Leaders Are Surprised When Collapse Comes

When collapse finally arrives, leaders are confused.

From their perspective:

- Orders were followed

- Authority was maintained

- Outcomes were pursued

What they miss is that **trust expired earlier**.

Trust does not collapse loudly.
 It dissolves.

By the time rebellion, mutiny, or failure appears, the causal moment is long past.

This is why systems so often misdiagnose collapse as sudden.

It is never sudden.

It is deferred.

---

11. The Trojan Parallel (and the Shared Fate)

Importantly, this pattern is not exclusive to the Greeks.

Troy suffers the same dynamic.

Trojan civilians endure siege.
Warriors fight knowing the end is likely.
Leaders make decisions insulated from the full cost.

Moral injury exists on both sides.

This framework is not partisan.

It is diagnostic.

Wherever systems persist by exporting pain, people carry the burden—and eventually, the system loses the capacity to command belief.

---

12. Modern Systems, Identical Accounting

The failure pattern in *The Iliad* appears unchanged in modern contexts:

- Corporations that survive layoffs while employees internalize loss

- Governments that persist while citizens absorb consequences

- Militaries that function while soldiers carry moral injury

- Institutions that remain respected while trust erodes

Metrics remain strong.
Performance continues.

Until it doesn't.

---

13. Strategic Implication (Without Prescription)

This framework does not suggest eliminating cost asymmetry.

It does not argue that systems should feel pain.

It insists on recognition.

If cost is always paid by people, then:

- Moral injury must be assumed, not treated as anomaly

- Loyalty must be monitored beyond compliance

- Silence cannot be read as stability

- Endurance cannot be mistaken for belief

Ignoring these truths does not preserve order.

It delays reckoning.

Closing Position

The Iliad is not a story about heroic suffering.

It is a record of how suffering is **distributed**.

Systems survive.
 Leaders persist.
 Objectives advance.

And people pay.

Not all at once.
 Not loudly.
 Not visibly.

But continuously.

> **Systems do not collapse when people suffer.**
> **They collapse when people stop believing the suffering means anything.**

By the time that belief is gone, rebellion is no longer necessary.

The system is already empty.

Chapter 4

Cost Is Paid by People, Not Systems

Core Reality

**Systems absorb loss.
People internalize it.**

1. The Fundamental Accounting Error in All Systems

Every system tells itself the same lie:

That it bears the cost of its own decisions.

It does not.

Systems are designed to endure.
People are designed to feel.

That difference is not incidental—it is structural.

When a system fails, it does not bleed.
When a strategy miscalculates, it does not grieve.
When leadership fractures, it does not carry shame.

People do.

This chapter formalizes a principle that *The Iliad* demonstrates with brutal consistency:

> **Systems remain intact by transferring pain to individuals who cannot refuse it.**

The Greek war effort does not collapse when Achilles withdraws.

It continues.

The command structure remains.
The hierarchy remains.
The objective remains.

But the cost of dysfunction is quietly shifted onto those with the least agency.

---

2. How Systems "Absorb" Loss

From the outside, the Greek system appears resilient.

Losses are recorded.
Battles are fought.
Replacements are made.
Funerals occur.

The system persists.

This creates the illusion that the system is absorbing damage.

In reality, what is happening is **diffusion**.

Loss is spread thinly enough across individuals that no single failure triggers systemic alarm.

This is the AWH diagnostic:

> **Systems do not feel cumulative loss.**
> **People do.**

Each death matters to someone.
Each humiliation lands somewhere.
Each moral compromise leaves residue.

The system logs numbers.
Humans carry memory.

---

3. The Silent Accumulation of Moral Injury

Moral injury is not trauma in the conventional sense.

It is not fear.
It is not shock.
It is not panic.

It is the internal conflict that arises when individuals are required to:

- Participate in injustice

- Endure preventable loss

- Obey decisions that violate internal standards

- Watch leaders protect status at the expense of others

In *The Iliad*, moral injury accumulates quietly.

Greek soldiers die not because Troy overwhelms them—but because Achilles is absent.

They know why he is absent.
 They know the dispute.
 They know it is personal.

And they die anyway.

This is the most corrosive form of injury:

To suffer for reasons you know are avoidable—and powerless to stop.

The system does not register this as failure.

But loyalty does.

4. Why Moral Injury Compounds Silently

Moral injury rarely produces immediate rebellion.

It produces compliance.

People continue to fight.
 They follow orders.
 They suppress resentment.

Because rebellion is costly.
 Because dissent is dangerous.
 Because systems punish disruption more reliably than they prevent harm.

So the injury compounds.

Each additional loss confirms a pattern:

- That leadership disputes matter more than lives

- That hierarchy is insulated from consequence

- That sacrifice is expected downward, never upward

This is why moral injury is so dangerous.

It does not announce itself.
 It waits.

5. The Mistake of Measuring Loyalty by Obedience

Systems routinely confuse obedience with loyalty.

They are not the same.

Obedience is enforced.
Loyalty is voluntary.

In *The Iliad*, Greek soldiers obey orders long after loyalty has begun to erode.

They fight without Achilles.
They accept losses.
They endure.

But something has already changed.

They no longer believe the system protects them.
They no longer believe sacrifice is reciprocal.
They no longer believe leadership bears cost alongside them.

This is the AWH warning:

When loyalty erodes, obedience becomes brittle.

The system cannot see this erosion because it does not show up in metrics.

Until it does.

---

6. Why Systems Miss the Point of Failure

Systems are designed to detect overt threats:

- Mutiny

- Defection

- Sabotage

- Open dissent

Moral injury produces none of these—at first.

It produces:

- Emotional withdrawal

- Reduced initiative

- Silent compliance

- Cynicism

- Loss of identification with mission

By the time rebellion appears, the system is already hollow.

The Iliad captures this perfectly.

The Greek army does not rebel against Agamemnon.
It simply **fails more often**.

Battles become bloodier.
Confidence erodes.
Heroes die unnecessarily.

The system interprets this as misfortune.

It is not.

It is delayed consequence.

---

7. Cost Displacement as a Survival Mechanism

It is important to be precise here.

Systems do not displace cost accidentally.

They do it **to survive**.

If leaders internalized every loss, no system would function.
If hierarchy collapsed under moral weight, coordination would
cease.

Cost displacement is not evil.
 It is structural.

But it has limits.

When too much cost is displaced downward, the system loses the very people it depends on—not through defection, but through disengagement.

Achilles' withdrawal is only the most visible example.

The quieter collapse happens among unnamed soldiers whose deaths are recorded but not remembered.

---

8. The Role of Leaders in Cost Asymmetry

Leadership magnifies cost asymmetry.

Leaders make decisions.
 Others pay for them.

This is not inherently unjust.
 It is unavoidable.

What becomes destructive is **lack of reciprocity**.

In *The Iliad*, Agamemnon's authority is never personally endangered by the losses he causes.

Achilles' authority is wounded symbolically—but not materially.

Greek soldiers absorb the full physical cost.

This asymmetry becomes intolerable when it is perceived as:

- Unnecessary

- Arbitrary

- Ego-driven

At that point, moral injury accelerates.

---

9. Loyalty Erodes Before Rebellion Appears

This is the most important warning in this chapter.

Rebellion is not the first sign of collapse.

It is the last.

Before rebellion, there is:

- Detachment

- Resignation

- Quiet resentment

- Emotional exit

People stop believing the system deserves them.

They still show up.
They still perform.
They still comply.

But the bond is broken.

The Iliad shows this erosion through atmosphere rather than declaration.

The war grows darker.
Deaths become heavier.
Honor feels hollow.

The system still functions.

But it no longer inspires.

---

10. Why Leaders Are Surprised When Collapse Comes

When collapse finally arrives, leaders are confused.

From their perspective:

- Orders were followed

- Authority was maintained

- Outcomes were pursued

What they miss is that **trust expired earlier**.

Trust does not collapse loudly.
It dissolves.

By the time rebellion, mutiny, or failure appears, the causal moment is long past.

This is why systems so often misdiagnose collapse as sudden.

It is never sudden.

It is deferred.

---

11. The Trojan Parallel (and the Shared Fate)

Importantly, this pattern is not exclusive to the Greeks.

Troy suffers the same dynamic.

Trojan civilians endure siege.
Warriors fight knowing the end is likely.
Leaders make decisions insulated from the full cost.

Moral injury exists on both sides.

This framework is not partisan.

It is diagnostic.

Wherever systems persist by exporting pain, people carry the burden—and eventually, the system loses the capacity to command belief.

---

12. Modern Systems, Identical Accounting

The failure pattern in *The Iliad* appears unchanged in modern contexts:

- Corporations that survive layoffs while employees internalize loss

- Governments that persist while citizens absorb consequences

- Militaries that function while soldiers carry moral injury

- Institutions that remain respected while trust erodes

Metrics remain strong.
 Performance continues.

Until it doesn't.

---

13. Strategic Implication (Without Prescription)

This framework does not suggest eliminating cost asymmetry.

It does not argue that systems should feel pain.

It insists on recognition.

If cost is always paid by people, then:

- Moral injury must be assumed, not treated as anomaly

- Loyalty must be monitored beyond compliance

- Silence cannot be read as stability

- Endurance cannot be mistaken for belief

Ignoring these truths does not preserve order.

It delays reckoning.

Closing Position

The Iliad is not a story about heroic suffering.

It is a record of how suffering is **distributed**.

Systems survive.
 Leaders persist.
 Objectives advance.

And people pay.

Not all at once.
 Not loudly.
 Not visibly.

But continuously.

> **Systems do not collapse when people suffer.**
> **They collapse when people stop believing the**
> **suffering means anything.**

By the time that belief is gone, rebellion is no longer necessary.

The system is already empty.

PART II

THE HUMAN PRIMITIVES

Irreducible Forces That Shape Collective Failure

Chapter 5

Pride

Misread

Pride is not arrogance—it is self-preservation.

---

1. Why Pride Must Be Treated as Primitive

This framework now moves beneath strategy.

Part I examined how systems fail *through* people.
Part II examines why those people behave in ways systems cannot control.

These are not learned behaviors.
They are not cultural artifacts.
They are not ideological distortions.

They are **primitives**—irreducible human forces that persist regardless of education, training, or structure.

Pride is the first.

Not because it is the loudest.
But because it is the most misunderstood.

Modern systems talk about pride as if it were optional.
As if it could be moderated, disciplined, or removed with enough professionalism.

The Iliad makes clear that this belief is fantasy.

Pride is not a personality trait.
It is an **identity defense system**.

When threatened, it activates automatically.
When ignored, it escalates.
When constrained, it resists.

This chapter formalizes the AWH position:

> **Pride is not excess confidence.**
> **It is the instinct to prevent erasure.**

2. Pride as Identity Defense

To understand pride, one must discard the moral frame.

Pride is not about superiority.
It is about **continuity of self**.

At its core, pride answers a single question:

Will I still exist as myself after this?

In *The Iliad*, Achilles' pride is not wounded because Agamemnon is rude.

It is wounded because Agamemnon's act threatens to redefine Achilles' identity within the system.

Briseis is not taken in private.
She is taken publicly.
Formally.
As precedent.

The message is not "you lose a prize."
The message is "your status is contingent."

Pride activates at this moment because identity is under threat.

This is the first correction this framework insists upon:

Pride emerges where identity feels unstable—not where arrogance exists.

3. Why Pride Is Triggered by Hierarchy

Pride is inseparable from hierarchy.

Not because humans love rank—but because rank determines meaning.

Every hierarchy answers:

- Who matters

- Who decides

- Who is protected

- Who is expendable

Pride activates when an individual perceives that the hierarchy no longer reflects their internal valuation of self.

Achilles believes his contribution entitles him to recognition.
 Agamemnon believes his position entitles him to dominance.

Both are defending identity.
 Both are defending coherence.

The conflict is not moral.
 It is structural.

This is why pride cannot be resolved by facts.

Facts do not restore identity.
 Hierarchy does.

---

4. Pride as Resistance to Hierarchy

Pride does not always seek dominance.

Often, it seeks **refusal**.

Achilles does not attempt to overthrow Agamemnon.
 He does not challenge the kingship.
 He does not rally rebellion.

He withdraws.

Withdrawal is pride's most disciplined form.

It says:

- *I will not be erased*

- *I will not validate this structure with my participation*

- *You may proceed without me—but not through me*

This is why pride is so destabilizing to systems.

It does not attack authority directly.
 It undermines it by removing voluntary alignment.

Systems interpret this as insubordination.
It is not.

It is **identity preservation under constraint**.

---

5. Why Pride Resists Correction

Correction assumes shared goals.

Pride assumes threatened existence.

When Odysseus, Phoenix, and Ajax attempt to persuade Achilles,
they appeal to:

- Logic

- Friendship

- Future reward

- Shared victory

All fail.

Not because Achilles is unreasonable.
But because accepting their arguments would require **accepting
the injury as legitimate**.

This is a core AWH diagnostic:

To accept correction is to accept the hierarchy as valid.

Pride refuses that concession.

---

6. Pride as Escalation Trigger

Pride does not seek conflict.
 But it escalates rapidly once threatened.

Why?

Because delay feels dangerous.

If an identity threat is not confronted immediately, it risks becoming normalized.

Achilles' withdrawal escalates the war—not by aggression, but by absence.

Agamemnon's refusal to yield escalates the conflict—not by force, but by rigidity.

Each escalation is defensive.

This is critical:

**Pride-driven escalation is not about winning.
It is about preventing permanent diminishment.**

Once escalation begins, compromise becomes harder—not easier—because each step backward feels like confirmation of weakness.

---

7. The Systemic Misread of Pride

Systems consistently misread pride in three ways:

1. **As arrogance**

2. **As emotional immaturity**

3. **As defiance to be disciplined**

Each misread worsens the situation.

Calling pride arrogance delegitimizes the grievance.
 Calling it immaturity infantilizes the actor.
 Calling it defiance escalates control.

None address the underlying issue: **identity threat within hierarchy**.

This is why systems often provoke the very escalation they seek to avoid.

---

8. Pride and the Illusion of Replaceability

Systems rely on a dangerous assumption:

That individuals are replaceable.

At a functional level, this is often true.

At an identity level, it is catastrophic.

Achilles is not replaceable—not because no one can fight like him, but because his presence **organizes meaning** for the system.

When pride is injured, withdrawal exposes how much the system depended on what it pretended was optional.

This pattern repeats everywhere:

- Founders

- Generals

- Creatives

- Cultural leaders

Replaceability is a logistical concept.
Pride operates on a symbolic one.

Confusing the two produces collapse.

9. Pride Does Not Fade With Time

One of the most persistent errors systems make is waiting.

They assume pride will cool.
That time will soften resistance.
That distance will restore cooperation.

The Iliad proves the opposite.

Pride does not decay without acknowledgment.
It hardens.

Each additional loss suffered in Achilles' absence confirms his stance.

Each ignored appeal strengthens identity separation.

Time does not heal pride injuries.
It **clarifies them**.

10. Pride and Moral Language

Systems often attempt to neutralize pride with morality.

They accuse the proud of:

- Selfishness

- Disloyalty

- Endangering others

These accusations miss the point.

Pride is not moral calculation.
 It is survival logic.

Achilles accepts the deaths of comrades not because he is
cruel—but because conceding would annihilate his self-definition.

This is uncomfortable.
 It is also real.

Moral language does not penetrate pride.
 It intensifies resistance by reframing identity defense as sin.

---

11. Pride as Collective Force

Pride is not confined to individuals.

Groups develop pride.
 Institutions develop pride.
 Nations develop pride.

When collective pride is injured, entire systems behave irrationally by strategic standards—and perfectly rationally by identity standards.

The Iliad is filled with collective pride:

- Greek honor

- Trojan defiance

- Warrior reputation

These forces prolong the war long after logic suggests resolution.

This framework insists:

Collective pride scales individual failure.

What is survivable at the personal level becomes catastrophic at the systemic one.

---

12. Why Pride Cannot Be Removed

Modern thinking often seeks solutions:

- Emotional intelligence

- Training

- Culture change

- Policy enforcement

These approaches assume pride is optional.

It is not.

Pride is the mechanism that prevents individuals from dissolving into systems entirely.

Without pride, humans would comply perfectly.
 They would also cease to be human.

The problem is not pride's existence.

It is systems that pretend pride does not exist—and are shocked when it asserts itself.

---

13. Strategic Implication (Without Prescription)

This framework does not advise leaders to cater to pride.
 It does not recommend appeasement.
 It does not offer ego management techniques.

It offers diagnosis.

If pride is a primitive, then:

- It will activate under threat

- It will resist hierarchy that negates identity

- It will escalate when ignored

- It will outlast logic and incentive

Planning that assumes otherwise is incomplete.

Closing Position

The Iliad does not depict pride as a tragic flaw.

It depicts pride as **the immune system of identity**.

Achilles is not arrogant.
 Agamemnon is not uniquely vain.

They are human.

Their pride is not what destroys the system.

The system is destroyed because it treats pride as a defect instead of a force.

> **Pride is not the enemy of order.**
> **Ignoring pride is.**

Part II begins here because until pride is understood as primitive and irreducible, every attempt at coordination, hierarchy, and strategy will fail in the same way Troy fell—

Not from lack of power.
 Not from lack of planning.
 But from misreading what humans will not surrender, even at catastrophic cost.

Chapter 6

Honor

Rule

Private compensation cannot repair public injury.

---

1. Why Honor Must Be Treated as Currency

Modern systems speak about honor as if it were symbolic.

Ancient systems did not.

In *The Iliad*, honor is not abstract virtue.
It is **currency**.

It determines:

- Who speaks and is heard

- Who commands and is obeyed

- Who is remembered and who disappears

* Who may suffer loss without protest

Honor circulates publicly.
It is visible.
It is comparative.
And it is finite.

This chapter formalizes a foundational AWH reality:

> **Honor is not what you feel about yourself.
> It is what the system publicly acknowledges
> about you.**

Where honor is mishandled, systems fracture—not because
people become immoral, but because the **exchange rate
collapses**.

---

2. Honor as Social Currency, Not Moral Value

To misunderstand honor as morality is to miss its function.

Honor does not measure goodness.
It measures **standing**.

In the Homeric world, honor is conferred through:

* Public recognition

- Allocation of prizes

- Verbal acknowledgment

- Ritual precedence

These signals form a ledger.

Everyone can see it.
 Everyone knows where they stand.

Achilles' rage does not erupt because he loses property.

It erupts because the public ledger is altered against him.

Agamemnon's seizure of Briseis is not theft.

It is **devaluation**.

This distinction is critical.

> **Material loss can be compensated.**
> **Honor loss changes identity.**

---

3. Why Honor Violations Outweigh Material Loss

Material loss affects resources.
 Honor loss affects **existence within the group**.

A warrior can recover wealth.
He cannot easily recover standing once it is publicly diminished.

This is why Achilles rejects compensation.

Agamemnon offers gold, women, territory, and future glory.

All irrelevant.

Why?

Because none reverse the **public meaning** of the original act.

The honor violation occurred in front of witnesses.
It redefined hierarchy.
It altered precedent.

Until that is repaired publicly, no private gain matters.

This produces one of the most misunderstood dynamics in *The Iliad*:

> **Achilles' refusal is not greed or petulance.**
> **It is economic rationality within an honor-based system.**

---

4. Honor and the Problem of Precedent

Honor violations are dangerous because they establish precedent.

If Agamemnon can seize Achilles' prize without consequence, then:

- No achievement guarantees recognition

- No contribution ensures protection

- No rank is secure

The injury is not isolated.
It is **systemic**.

Achilles understands this immediately.

His withdrawal is not just protest.
It is refusal to legitimize a new, degraded exchange rate for honor.

This is the AWH diagnostic:

> **Honor disputes are never about the past.**
> **They are about the future rules of valuation.**

---

5. Why Honor Demands Public Repair

Because honor is public, repair must be public.

Private apologies fail.
Private compensation fails.
Private understanding fails.

Agamemnon's emissaries misunderstand this completely.

They negotiate as if the issue were transactional.
They speak as if Achilles were angry about loss.

He is angry about **meaning**.

AWH formalizes the rule:

> **Public injury requires public repair.**
> **Anything less confirms the insult.**

Repair must:

- Acknowledge the violation openly

- Recalibrate hierarchy visibly

- Restore symbolic standing

- Signal new limits on authority

Agamemnon does none of this.

He apologizes, but he does not submit.
He compensates, but he does not reverse the signal.
He remains king—unchallenged.

The injury persists.

---

6. Honor vs. Authority: The Hidden Conflict

Systems often confuse authority with honor.

They are not the same.

Authority is positional.
 Honor is relational.

Agamemnon has authority.
 Achilles has honor.

The system assumes authority should override honor.

The Iliad proves the opposite.

Authority that disregards honor creates resistance that authority cannot compel away.

Achilles does not rebel.
 He does not attack the hierarchy.

He simply stops participating in it.

This reveals a hard truth:

> **Honor is the voluntary substrate beneath authority.**
> **When it is withdrawn, authority hollows out.**

7. Why Honor Cannot Be Repaired Quietly

Modern systems are allergic to spectacle.

They prefer:

- Quiet settlements

- Back-channel apologies

- Confidential compensation

This works in material disputes.

It fails catastrophically in honor disputes.

Why?

Because the audience matters.

Honor is not exchanged between two parties.
It is exchanged **in front of witnesses**.

Those witnesses update their understanding of the system based on what they see.

If repair is hidden, the original injury remains the last public signal.

This is why Achilles' stance hardens rather than softens over time.

Nothing public changes.

8. Honor and the Audience Effect

Honor only exists because there is an audience.

Greek warriors watch Achilles.
They watch Agamemnon.
They watch the exchange.

They learn:

- Who can be humiliated

- Who cannot

- What excellence is worth

- Whether merit protects you

When Achilles withdraws, the audience learns something else:

That honor, once violated, is defended even at catastrophic cost.

This lesson spreads silently.

Systems underestimate this diffusion.

They believe disputes are contained.

They are not.

9. The Cost of Honor Violations Is Always Displaced

As established in Chapter 4, systems displace cost downward.

Honor violations accelerate this displacement.

Achilles' injury is symbolic.
 The cost is paid in blood—by others.

This creates a second-order injury:

Those who suffer begin to understand that their lives are collateral in honor disputes they did not choose.

This compounds moral injury.
 Loyalty erodes faster.
 Cynicism deepens.

The system persists.
 Belief does not.

10. Why Honor Is So Resistant to Rational Framing

Honor does not respond to logic because it does not operate in the same domain.

Logic optimizes outcomes.
Honor preserves identity within a group.

Achilles is repeatedly told:

- The war matters more

- The Greeks need him

- Lives are at stake

He does not disagree.

He simply refuses to accept a reality where his standing is negotiable.

This produces the uncomfortable AWH conclusion:

> **Honor can make catastrophic loss acceptable if identity is preserved.**

This is not madness.
It is priority ordering.

---

11. Honor and Escalation Dynamics

Honor disputes escalate predictably.

Stage 1: Public injury
Stage 2: Private attempts at repair

Stage 3: Rejection
Stage 4: Cost displacement
Stage 5: Irreversible loss

The Iliad follows this sequence precisely.

The tragedy is not that escalation occurs.

It is that the system **never addresses the right layer**.

---

12. Why Systems Repeatedly Misread Honor

Systems misread honor because acknowledging it threatens hierarchy.

To repair honor publicly often requires:

- Admission of overreach

- Visible concession

- Temporary status reversal

Authority resists this instinctively.

It prefers material compensation and rhetorical apology.

These preserve structure.
They fail to restore meaning.

The system believes it has been generous.
The injured party experiences confirmation of disrespect.

---

13. Modern Parallels of the Same Failure

Honor has not disappeared.

It has changed form.

Modern honor appears as:

- Reputation

- Credibility

- Visibility

- Credit

- Public acknowledgment

The same failure pattern repeats when:

- Contributions are erased

- Credit is reassigned

- Authority humiliates publicly

- Repair is attempted quietly

The language changes.
The dynamic does not.

---

14. Strategic Implication (Without Prescription)

This framework does not instruct leaders to stage public contrition.
It does not advise ritual apology.
It does not recommend symbolic theater.

It diagnoses reality.

If honor is social currency, then:

- Public injury cannot be repaired privately

- Material compensation cannot substitute for recognition

- Authority cannot nullify honor without consequence

- Silence after injury is escalation, not neutrality

Ignoring these truths does not produce stability.

It produces delayed collapse.

Closing Position

The Iliad is not driven by greed.
It is not driven by vengeance.
It is not driven by fate.

It is driven by **broken honor economies**.

Achilles' rage is not excess emotion.

It is the rational response of an actor whose currency has been publicly devalued—and whose system refuses to acknowledge the exchange.

> **Honor is not fragile because it is emotional.**
> **It is fragile because it is public.**

And when public injury is met with private repair, the message is clear:

The system would rather preserve hierarchy than meaning.

At that point, escalation is not chosen.

It is inevitable.

Chapter 7

Status

Core Reality

Status determines voice, not rank.
Unequal recognition breeds withdrawal.

---

1. Why Status Must Be Distinguished From Rank

Most systems collapse because they confuse two different concepts:

- **Rank**: formal position within a hierarchy

- **Status**: perceived value within the collective

Rank is assigned.
Status is conferred.

Rank is static.
Status is dynamic.

Rank can be enforced.
Status must be recognized.

This distinction is not semantic.
It is structural.

In *The Iliad*, Agamemnon outranks Achilles.
No one disputes this.

But Achilles possesses greater **status**.

He is the most effective warrior.
He carries the war's momentum.
His presence alters outcomes.

The system assumes rank should override status.

This assumption is fatal.

This chapter formalizes a central AWH principle:

> **Rank can compel obedience.**
> **Only status compels participation.**

---

2. Status as the Gatekeeper of Voice

Voice is not distributed equally in systems.

It is not allocated by title.
It is granted by status.

Who is listened to?
Who can dissent without punishment?
Who can refuse without expulsion?

These questions are answered by status, not rank.

Achilles speaks with authority because others accept his valuation of himself.
Agamemnon speaks with authority because the hierarchy supports him.

When these authorities collide, the system must choose which it privileges.

In *The Iliad*, it chooses rank.

The consequence is silence.

Achilles does not argue endlessly.
He withdraws.

This is the first warning sign systems miss:

> **When high-status actors stop speaking, collapse has already begun.**

---

3. Why Status Loss Is More Dangerous Than Status Competition

Systems often expect rivalry.

They are less prepared for **status loss**.

Status competition produces friction.
 Status loss produces disengagement.

Achilles is not fighting Agamemnon for higher status.
 He is responding to **status degradation**.

The seizure of Briseis does not elevate Agamemnon meaningfully.
 It lowers Achilles publicly.

That asymmetry matters.

Status loss communicates:

- Your contribution is conditional

- Your excellence is negotiable

- Your standing is insecure

Once this message is sent, cooperation becomes irrational.

This is not pride.
 It is **risk management**.

---

4. Status Loss Destabilizes Coalitions

Coalitions rely on alignment between contribution and recognition.

When this alignment breaks, coalitions do not fracture immediately.

They hollow out.

The Greek coalition does not dissolve when Achilles withdraws. It continues to function structurally.

But its most powerful contributor is gone.

This reveals a core AWH diagnostic:

> **Coalitions rarely collapse through defection.**
> **They collapse through withdrawal.**

Status loss incentivizes withdrawal because it allows individuals to:

- Preserve dignity

- Avoid legitimizing devaluation

- Maintain identity coherence

Withdrawal is quieter than rebellion.
It is also more destructive.

5. Why Unequal Recognition Breeds Withdrawal

Recognition is not about praise.
 It is about proportionality.

Achilles does not demand special treatment.
 He demands **consistent valuation**.

When the system violates that consistency, it signals unpredictability.

Unequal recognition tells contributors:

- Effort does not guarantee standing

- Sacrifice does not ensure respect

- Excellence does not protect you

In such systems, continued participation becomes a gamble.

Achilles opts out.

This is not sabotage.
 It is **rational disengagement**.

6. Status and the Illusion of Replaceability

Systems tell themselves that no one is indispensable.

At the logistical level, this is often true.
 At the symbolic level, it is not.

Status is not about function.
 It is about meaning.

Achilles' absence exposes this illusion brutally.

The Greeks can fight without him.
 They cannot fight **well** without him.

Status loss reveals dependency systems deny until it is too late.

---

7. Why Status Conflicts Are Misdiagnosed as Ego Problems

Modern systems often mislabel status conflicts as ego clashes.

This is convenient.
 It individualizes the problem.

But status conflicts are not psychological.
 They are structural.

Achilles' behavior changes not because his personality shifts, but because the system's valuation of him does.

This is the AWH correction:

> **When behavior changes after recognition changes, the issue is status—not ego.**

Treating status loss as ego inflation ensures misdiagnosis and failed repair.

---

8. Status Asymmetry and Moral Injury

Status loss does not only affect the injured party.

It affects observers.

Greek soldiers watch Achilles be diminished.
They watch Agamemnon assert dominance.
They update their understanding of the system.

They learn:

- Excellence is not protected

- Authority is arbitrary

- Sacrifice is one-sided

This produces moral injury at scale.

Loyalty erodes quietly.
Trust thins.
Belief weakens.

The coalition still exists.
Its spirit does not.

---

9. Why Status Loss Cannot Be Corrected Quietly

As with honor, status is public.

Loss occurs in front of witnesses.
Repair must as well.

Private negotiation fails because it does not update the public ledger.

Agamemnon's offers to Achilles misunderstand this completely.

They assume status loss can be offset materially.

It cannot.

Status is comparative.
It is visible.
It is zero-sum in perception.

This produces the hard rule of this chapter:

---

10. The Role of Witnesses in Status Dynamics

Status does not exist in isolation.

It exists because others see and agree.

The audience matters.

Every Greek warrior who watches Achilles' humiliation becomes a
witness.
 Every witness updates their internal map of the hierarchy.

This is why status disputes spread.

They are not contained between two individuals.
 They recalibrate the entire coalition.

Systems consistently underestimate this diffusion effect.

---

11. Status and Escalation Without Intent

One of the most dangerous aspects of status loss is that it
escalates systems **without conscious intent**.

Achilles does not set out to destabilize the Greek war effort.
 Agamemnon does not set out to fracture the coalition.

Both act to preserve status.

The escalation emerges as a secondary effect.

This is why status must be treated as a primitive force.

It does not require malice.
 It does not require incompetence.
 It only requires misalignment.

---

12. Modern Systems, Same Failure Pattern

Status dynamics did not disappear with ancient warfare.

They appear wherever:

- Credit is unevenly distributed

- Authority overrides contribution

- Visibility is manipulated

- Recognition is politicized

Modern equivalents include:

- Founders sidelined after growth

- Executives stripped of influence publicly

- Creators erased from their own work

- High performers ignored while authority consolidates

The language changes.
The response does not.

Withdrawal follows.

---

13. Strategic Implication (Without Prescription)

This framework does not recommend flattening hierarchies.
It does not advise constant affirmation.
It does not suggest appeasement.

It diagnoses reality.

If status determines voice, then:

- Silencing high-status contributors is destabilizing

- Unequal recognition incentivizes disengagement

- Rank cannot substitute for legitimacy

- Coalitions weaken long before they fracture

Ignoring these truths produces systems that appear strong until they suddenly are not.

Closing Position

The Iliad does not show a coalition destroyed by enemies.

It shows a coalition undone by **status mismanagement**.

Achilles does not betray the Greeks.
He simply refuses to validate a system that no longer recognizes him proportionally.

This is the final, uncomfortable truth of status:

> **People do not leave systems when they are defeated.**
> **They leave when they are diminished.**

By the time withdrawal is visible, the coalition has already lost what made it formidable.

Not its numbers.
Not its weapons.
But its belief that contribution and recognition still align.

And no system survives that loss for long.

Chapter 8

Loyalty

Core Reality

**Loyalty is conditional, not permanent.
Loyalty responds to treatment, not rhetoric.
Betrayal often begins as silence.**

---

1. The Myth of Permanent Loyalty

Every system believes it has loyalty.

It counts tenure.
It counts past sacrifice.
It counts declared allegiance.

And from these counts, it draws a dangerous conclusion:

That loyalty, once earned, persists on its own.

The Iliad refutes this assumption without argument.

Loyalty in the poem is not eternal.
It is **situational, contingent, and responsive.**

Greek warriors are loyal—until they are not.
 Allies fight—until they withdraw.
 Even the gods shift allegiances based on treatment, recognition, and insult.

This chapter establishes a foundational AWH principle:

> **Loyalty is not stored.**
> **It is renewed—or depleted—through experience.**

Systems that misunderstand this do not lose loyalty suddenly.

They lose it **quietly, invisibly, and irreversibly**.

---

2. What Loyalty Actually Is

Loyalty is often framed as devotion.

It is not.

Loyalty is a **cost-benefit alignment filtered through identity and treatment**.

At its most basic level, loyalty answers three questions:

1. *Does this system recognize me appropriately?*

2. *Does it protect me proportionally to my sacrifice?*

3. *Does my continued participation preserve or diminish my identity?*

When the answers trend negative, loyalty erodes—even if rhetoric remains positive.

In *The Iliad*, Greek warriors continue to fight for Agamemnon long after Achilles withdraws.

This is not loyalty.

It is **obedience under constraint**.

True loyalty—the kind that produces discretionary effort, risk-taking, and resilience—has already begun to thin.

---

3. Loyalty Is Conditional, Not Moral

Modern systems often moralize loyalty.

They describe it as:

- Faithfulness

- Commitment

- Character

- Integrity

This framing is strategically disastrous.

Because once loyalty is moralized, its erosion is interpreted as **sin rather than signal**.

The Iliad treats loyalty differently.

Loyalty shifts in response to:

- Treatment

- Recognition

- Fairness

- Honor distribution

Achilles is loyal to the Greek cause—until the cause no longer treats him as integral.

His withdrawal is not treason.
It is **conditional disengagement**.

This is the AWH correction:

> **Loyalty is not a moral state.**
> **It is a relational response.**

4. Loyalty Responds to Treatment, Not Rhetoric

One of the most persistent failures in leadership systems is speech.

Leaders believe words can repair what actions damaged.

They invoke:

- Shared mission

- Past sacrifice

- Collective destiny

- Moral obligation

In *The Iliad*, every one of these appeals is made to Achilles.

All fail.

Why?

Because loyalty does not respond to **what is said**.

It responds to **what is experienced**.

Agamemnon speaks of unity.
His actions communicate disposability.

The words cannot override the treatment.

This produces a hard rule this chapter insists upon:

Rhetoric cannot outpace behavior without accelerating disengagement.

When words and treatment diverge, loyalty collapses faster—not slower.

---

5. The Illusion of Loyalty During Crisis

Crises create a dangerous illusion.

When external threat is high, people remain engaged even under poor treatment.

Systems misinterpret this as loyalty.

It is not.

It is **threat compression**.

In *The Iliad*, the Greek army remains cohesive during intense Trojan pressure—even without Achilles.

Leaders conclude the system is holding.

It is not.

What is happening is temporary alignment driven by fear and survival.

Once the pressure stabilizes, underlying fractures surface.

This is why loyalty failures often appear **after** crises—not during them.

---

6. How Loyalty Quietly Erodes

Loyalty does not disappear with drama.

It dissolves through accumulation.

Small signals matter:

- Ignored contributions

- Unacknowledged sacrifice

- Unequal punishment

- Arbitrary authority

- Symbolic humiliation

None individually trigger rebellion.

Together, they produce disengagement.

In *The Iliad*, no single act breaks loyalty at scale.

But patterns do.

Greek warriors observe:

- Achilles humiliated

- Agamemnon insulated

- Losses displaced downward

They draw conclusions quietly.

This is the AWH warning:

Loyalty erodes long before behavior changes.

---

7. Betrayal Often Begins as Silence

Systems are trained to watch for betrayal.

They monitor:

- Open dissent

- Defection

- Sabotage

- Resistance

They are blind to **silence**.

Silence is loyalty withdrawing without confrontation.

Achilles' silence after his withdrawal is more dangerous than open rebellion.

He does not argue.
He does not negotiate endlessly.
He does not disrupt command.

He simply stops contributing.

This is the most lethal form of disengagement.

Why?

Because it preserves legitimacy while draining capability.

Systems consistently misread silence as compliance.

It is not.

It is **exit without departure**.

---

8. Why Silence Is Chosen Over Rebellion

Rebellion is costly.

It invites punishment.
It clarifies sides.
It forces confrontation.

Silence avoids all three.

For high-status contributors, silence is often the optimal response to mistreatment.

It allows:

- Identity preservation

- Dignified withdrawal

- Pressure without exposure

Achilles chooses silence because it:

- Protects his honor

- Preserves his autonomy

- Maximizes system discomfort

This is not spite.
It is **strategic non-participation**.

---

9. Loyalty and the Redistribution of Risk

Loyalty persists when risk and reward feel proportionate.

When risk is displaced downward and reward upward, loyalty
weakens.

In *The Iliad*:

- Leaders argue

- Warriors die

- Recognition flows unevenly

This asymmetry matters more than ideology.

People tolerate danger.
 They do not tolerate **expendability**.

This is why loyalty fractures even when objectives remain valid.

The cause does not fail.
 The relationship does.

---

10. Why Systems Misdiagnose Loyalty Collapse

When loyalty finally collapses, systems are shocked.

They say:

- "We never saw this coming."

- "They were committed."

- "Nothing had changed."

This is false.

Everything had changed.

What failed was **perception**.

Because systems measure loyalty through:

- Attendance

- Compliance

- Output

Instead of:

- Discretionary effort

- Willingness to speak

- Voluntary sacrifice

- Emotional identification

By the time these vanish, loyalty is already gone.

---

11. Loyalty Is Not Symmetrical

Another critical misunderstanding is symmetry.

Systems assume loyalty flows upward as much as downward.

It does not.

Subordinates are expected to be loyal.
 Leaders are expected to be effective.

When leaders fail in treatment, subordinates adjust loyalty.
 When subordinates fail, they are punished.

This asymmetry accelerates erosion.

In *The Iliad*, Agamemnon's failure costs others.
 Achilles' response costs the system.

The asymmetry is unsustainable.

---

12. The Moralization Trap

When loyalty erodes, systems moralize.

They accuse disengaged actors of:

- Disloyalty

- Selfishness

- Betrayal

- Weakness

This framing is comforting.
It absolves leadership.

It is also wrong.

Loyalty erosion is rarely moral failure.
It is **system feedback**.

Treating it as sin ensures repetition.

---

13. Modern Systems, Identical Pattern

The loyalty dynamics in *The Iliad* persist unchanged in modern
contexts:

- Employees disengage long before they quit

- Partners go silent before they leave

- Allies reduce support before they defect

- Citizens withdraw belief before they revolt

In every case, leadership is surprised.
In every case, the signals were present.
In every case, silence came first.

---

14. Strategic Implication (Without Prescription)

This framework does not offer loyalty-building tactics.
It does not suggest motivational language.
It does not recommend cultural slogans.

It diagnoses reality.

If loyalty is conditional, then:

- Past sacrifice does not guarantee future commitment

- Rhetoric cannot substitute for treatment

- Silence must be treated as warning

- Obedience cannot be confused with belief

Ignoring these truths does not preserve unity.

It delays recognition.

Closing Position

The Iliad does not portray loyalty as noble constancy.

It portrays loyalty as **fragile alignment**—maintained only so long as treatment, recognition, and identity remain intact.

Achilles does not betray the Greeks.
 He withdraws loyalty because loyalty is no longer reciprocated.

This is the final, uncomfortable truth this chapter leaves behind:

> **Betrayal rarely begins with opposition.**
> **It begins with silence.**

And systems that only listen for noise will never hear it coming.

Chapter 9

Grief

Key Insight

Grieving leaders do not optimize—they react.

---

1. Why Grief Belongs Among the Human Primitives

Grief is often treated as an emotional aftermath.

A response.
 A phase.
 Something to be endured privately and overcome quickly so that decision-making can "return to normal."

The Iliad does not treat grief this way.

It treats grief as **a force**.

A force strong enough to override hierarchy, logic, restraint, and even self-preservation.

Part II of this framework isolates the human primitives because they are **irreducible**. They cannot be trained away, rationalized out, or subordinated to procedure.

Grief is one of the most dangerous primitives because it:

- Appears justified

- Commands sympathy

- Masks escalation as inevitability

This chapter establishes the AWH position clearly:

> **Grief is not a temporary impairment.**
> **It is a full-system reconfiguration of priority,**
> **perception, and action.**

---

2. What Grief Actually Is (Structurally, Not Emotionally)

Grief is not sadness.

Sadness can coexist with strategy.
Grief cannot.

Grief is **the collapse of the assumed future**.

It is the sudden realization that:

- What mattered is gone

- What was expected will not occur

- What justified past sacrifice has dissolved

This collapse rewrites internal logic.

Before grief:

- Decisions optimize outcomes

- Trade-offs are evaluated

- Long-term consequences matter

After grief:

- Decisions seek relief

- Pain avoidance dominates

- The future compresses into the present

This is why grief is so destabilizing in leadership contexts.

It does not distort thinking randomly.
It **reorders objectives**.

---

3. Patroclus: The Moment the System Breaks

In *The Iliad*, the Greek war effort survives pride, honor disputes, and status fracture.

It does not survive grief.

Patroclus' death is not just a loss.
It is the **event horizon** of the poem.

Achilles does not merely return to battle.
He becomes something else.

> *"So spoke he, and black clouds of grief closed round him."*

This is not poetic flourish.
It is diagnostic language.

From this moment on:

- Restraint disappears

- Objectives narrow

- Proportionality collapses

The war changes character—not because Troy adapts, but because Achilles' internal state rewrites his behavior.

4. Loss Reshapes Priorities

Before grief, Achilles' priority is identity preservation.

After grief, identity becomes irrelevant.

This shift is critical.

Grief does not add a new priority.
It **destroys the old hierarchy of priorities entirely**.

Achilles no longer cares about:

- Honor economy

- Hierarchy

- Recognition

- Long-term consequence

He cares about:

- Immediate action

- Direct confrontation

- Pain externalization

This is the AWH diagnostic:

**Grief flattens priority structures.
Everything collapses into "now."**

Systems built on sequencing, patience, and restraint cannot survive this shift.

---

5. Why Grief Narrows Decision Horizons

Strategic decision-making requires time.

Not clock time—but **psychological time**.

Grief compresses time to the present moment.

The future feels irrelevant.
The past feels fixed and accusatory.
Only action now seems meaningful.

Achilles' response is immediate, absolute, and excessive.

He does not plan a campaign.
He does not negotiate terms.
He does not consider fallout.

He attacks.

This is not recklessness.
It is **temporal collapse**.

Grief eliminates the mental space required for optimization.

---

6. Grief Transforms Objectives

One of the most dangerous aspects of grief is that it does not simply intensify existing goals.

It **replaces them**.

Before Patroclus' death:

- The objective is victory

- The constraint is identity and honor

After Patroclus' death:

- The objective is expression of grief through destruction

- Victory becomes incidental

Hector's death does not advance the war strategically.
It satisfies a grief-driven need for confrontation and release.

This is the AWH insight that systems consistently miss:

Grief converts outcomes into symbols.
Success becomes emotional discharge, not
strategic gain.

---

7. Why Grief Is Often Misread as Resolve

From the outside, grief-driven leaders look decisive.

They act quickly.
They show intensity.
They inspire fear or awe.

Systems mistake this for clarity.

It is not.

It is **reactive certainty**—a dangerous substitute for judgment.

Achilles is more effective in combat after Patroclus' death.
He is also more destructive, less discriminating, and less governable.

Grief can temporarily increase output while permanently destroying alignment.

---

8. Grief and the Loss of Constraint

Before grief, Achilles still observes limits.

After grief, limits dissolve.

He mutilates Hector's body.
He rejects appeals for mercy.
He defies ritual norms.

> *"I wish my fury would drive me now*
> *to hack your flesh away and eat you raw."*

This is not cruelty for cruelty's sake.

It is grief overriding boundary recognition.

Grief removes the internal brakes that allow leaders to remain predictable within systems.

This is why grieving leaders are so dangerous—not because they are evil, but because they are **uncontained**.

---

9. Why Advice Fails in the Presence of Grief

After Patroclus' death, no one persuades Achilles.

Not Thetis.
Not Priam.
Not the memory of consequences.

Advice presumes:

- Shared objectives

- Future orientation

- Emotional capacity to receive input

Grief negates all three.

This is why systems that continue to offer counsel to grieving leaders misinterpret silence or aggression as defiance rather than incapacity.

> **Grief is not resistance to advice.**
> **It is inability to integrate it.**

---

10. Grief as Contagion

Grief is not isolated.

It spreads.

Patroclus' death reshapes Achilles.
Achilles' response reshapes the war.
The war reshapes everyone within it.

Grief propagates through:

- Escalation

- Excess violence

- Retaliation cycles

Each act generates new loss, producing more grief.

This is how systems spiral.

No one chooses escalation.
 They react to grief-induced behavior.

---

11. Why Grief Produces Overkill

Optimization seeks sufficiency.

Grief seeks **certainty**.

Achilles does not want Hector defeated.
 He wants Hector erased.

Overkill is grief's attempt to ensure finality—because grief cannot tolerate ambiguity.

This explains why grief-driven actions are often:

- Excessive

- Symbolic

- Irreversible

They are not about effectiveness.
They are about emotional closure.

---

12. The Illusion of Control During Grief

Leaders under grief often believe they are in control.

Their actions feel purposeful.
Their anger feels justified.
Their urgency feels necessary.

Systems reinforce this illusion because:

- Results may initially improve

- Fear produces compliance

- Momentum masks fragility

But control is gone.

The leader is no longer steering the system.
The system is being dragged by the leader's internal state.

---

13. Why Grief Is So Often Deferred, Not Addressed

Systems are uncomfortable with grief.

They prefer to:

- Rush past it

- Compartmentalize it

- Minimize it

- Weaponize it

They do not stop to recognize what grief actually does to decision-making.

In *The Iliad*, no mechanism exists to absorb Achilles' grief.

The system adapts by **allowing devastation**.

This is not a failure of compassion.
It is a failure of design.

---

14. Modern Systems, Same Failure Pattern

Grief-driven leadership is not ancient.

It appears whenever leaders experience:

- Personal loss

- Public humiliation

- Irrecoverable failure

- Symbolic death of legacy

Modern equivalents include:

- Leaders escalating conflict after loss

- Executives burning organizations after betrayal

- Political figures radicalizing after defeat

The language changes.
The dynamic does not.

Grief narrows horizons.
Objectives mutate.
Systems follow.

15. Strategic Implication (Without Prescription)

This framework does not advise grief counseling.
It does not recommend time off.
It does not propose emotional containment strategies.

It diagnoses reality.

If grieving leaders do not optimize, then:

- Expecting rational trade-offs is a category error

- Interpreting escalation as strategy is a mistake

- Assuming proportionality is dangerous

- Allowing grieving leaders unilateral power guarantees excess

Ignoring these truths does not produce resilience.

It produces catastrophe with momentum.

Closing Position

The Iliad does not present Achilles' grief as noble tragedy.

It presents it as **system-altering force**.

The war does not end because Achilles returns.
 It becomes more destructive.

Patroclus' death does not clarify purpose.
 It erases constraint.

This chapter closes with the hardest truth in this framework:

> **Grief is not a pause in leadership.**
> **It is a transformation of it.**

And systems that expect grieving leaders to continue optimizing
for outcomes will instead receive reaction, escalation, and
irreversible loss—
 long after the original objective has ceased to matter.

That is why grief belongs among the primitives.

Because once it enters the system,
 strategy no longer decides what happens next.

PART III

COALITION DYNAMICS

Why Alliances Collapse Internally

Chapter 10

Coalitions Are Fragile by Default

Core Realities

Multiple incentives coexist uneasily.
 Alignment requires constant maintenance.
 Shared enemies do not guarantee unity.

---

1. The Myth of the Stable Coalition

Most alliances are built on a comforting belief:

That once aligned, interests remain aligned.

This belief is false.

Coalitions are not natural states.
They are **temporary constructions**.

They exist only so long as:

- Incentives overlap

- Recognition feels proportionate

- Costs feel shared

- Identity remains intact

Remove any one of these, and cohesion begins to decay.

The Iliad is not a story of a coalition overwhelmed by an enemy.

It is a record of a coalition **rotting while winning**.

This chapter formalizes the AWH principle that governs all collective action:

Coalitions are fragile by default.
Stability is artificial and requires work.

---

2. Why Coalitions Exist at All

Coalitions form because single actors lack sufficient power.

They are born of necessity, not trust.

In *The Iliad*, the Greek coalition exists because:

- No single king can defeat Troy alone

- Resources must be pooled

- Prestige must be shared

This creates a temporary overlap of incentives.

But overlap is not unity.

Unity requires:

- Shared meaning

- Predictable recognition

- Managed hierarchy

Coalitions rarely invest in these.

They assume the enemy will do the work for them.

---

3. Multiple Incentives Coexist Uneasily

Every coalition contains **competing motivations**.

In the Greek alliance:

- Agamemnon seeks supremacy and authority

- Achilles seeks honor and recognition

- Other kings seek survival, prestige, and spoils

- Soldiers seek safety and meaning

These incentives do not cancel each other out.
They sit beside each other—uneasily.

This is the first structural weakness of coalitions:

They require people to act together for different reasons.

As long as incentives overlap, the coalition functions.

When pressure shifts, fractures appear.

---

4. Alignment Is Not Binary—It Is Gradual

Systems often treat alignment as on/off.

Aligned or misaligned.
United or divided.

Reality is gradient.

Coalitions drift before they break.

In *The Iliad*, alignment erodes slowly:

- First through status injury

- Then through honor violations

- Then through unequal cost distribution

- Finally through silence and withdrawal

By the time the coalition appears fractured, it has already failed internally.

This is the AWH diagnostic:

> **Coalitions do not collapse suddenly.**
> **They decay quietly while appearing intact.**

---

5. Why Shared Enemies Do Not Guarantee Unity

The most common coalition myth is externalization:

> **"As long as the enemy exists, we will stay united."**

The Iliad disproves this completely.

Troy remains.
 The threat persists.
 The war continues.

And yet the Greek coalition fractures anyway.

Why?

Because external threats do not resolve **internal disputes over value, status, and cost**.

Shared enemies create urgency.
 They do not create fairness.

Once survival is no longer immediately threatened, internal hierarchies come under scrutiny.

This is when coalitions become most unstable.

---

6. The False Comfort of External Pressure

External pressure masks internal problems.

When losses are high and danger is constant, dissent is suppressed.

Not resolved—suppressed.

In *The Iliad*, intense fighting delays internal reckoning.

Leaders interpret continued participation as loyalty.
 They are wrong.

What they are seeing is **constraint**, not commitment.

As pressure fluctuates, suppressed conflicts resurface with greater force.

This is why coalitions often collapse **after** major victories, not before them.

---

7. Coalition Maintenance Is Work—And No One Wants to Do It

Alignment does not sustain itself.

It requires:

- Continuous recognition

- Status calibration

- Cost acknowledgment

- Boundary enforcement

Coalitions rarely perform this maintenance because:

- It threatens authority

- It requires visible concessions

- It forces uncomfortable recalibration

Agamemnon does not maintain alignment.
He asserts dominance.

The result is not obedience.
It is disengagement.

This reveals a hard truth:

Coalitions fail not from malice, but from neglect.

---

8. Hierarchy Is Necessary—and Dangerous

Coalitions require hierarchy to function.

Someone must decide.
Someone must coordinate.
Someone must bear authority.

But hierarchy creates tension when:

- Authority is insulated from cost

- Recognition flows unevenly

- Rank overrides contribution

In *The Iliad*, hierarchy is not the problem.

Unmanaged hierarchy is.

Agamemnon's authority is legitimate.
His disregard for proportional recognition is destabilizing.

Coalitions collapse not because hierarchy exists—but because it is **left unchecked**.

---

9. Why Coalitions Misinterpret Silence

Coalitions watch for rebellion.

They monitor:

- Open dissent

- Defection

- Confrontation

They ignore silence.

Silence is interpreted as agreement.
It is not.

It is **unpaid attention withdrawing**.

Achilles' withdrawal is not loud.
It is devastating.

By the time silence becomes visible failure, the coalition has already lost its most valuable asset.

---

10. Unequal Cost Accelerates Coalition Breakdown

Coalitions survive only when cost feels proportionate.

When:

- Some decide

- Others suffer

- And recognition does not match sacrifice

alignment dissolves.

In *The Iliad*, soldiers die for disputes they did not create.

They observe:

- Leaders arguing

- Costs displaced downward

- Authority protected

This creates quiet resentment—not mutiny.

Coalitions do not collapse when cost is high.
 They collapse when cost feels **unfair**.

---

11. Why Coalitions Fail to Self-Correct

Once misalignment begins, coalitions face a dilemma:

Correct it—and risk authority.
 Ignore it—and risk collapse.

Most choose the latter.

Because misalignment is invisible until it is irreversible.

By the time leaders recognize coalition failure, the problem is framed as:

- Disloyalty

- Ego

- Betrayal

Instead of what it is:

Accumulated mismanagement of alignment.

---

12. The Trojan Side: Same Failure, Different Timing

The Trojan coalition exhibits the same fragility.

Allies support Troy for overlapping but divergent reasons. As losses mount and hope fades, commitment weakens.

Coalitions on both sides are fragile—not because of morality, but because **alignment degrades under prolonged pressure**.

This framework is not partisan.

It is structural.

---

13. Modern Coalitions, Identical Dynamics

The patterns in *The Iliad* appear unchanged in modern contexts:

- Corporate mergers that collapse post-integration

- Political alliances that fracture after elections

- Military coalitions that fail after early success

- Social movements that splinter once visibility rises

In every case:

- Incentives diverge

- Recognition skews

- Maintenance is neglected

Collapse follows.

---

14. Strategic Implication (Without Prescription)

This framework does not offer alliance-building tactics.
It does not propose unity slogans.
It does not recommend enemy framing.

It diagnoses reality.

If coalitions are fragile by default, then:

- Alignment must be treated as temporary

- Shared enemies cannot substitute for internal equity

- Silence must be read as risk

- Victory must not be mistaken for cohesion

Ignoring these truths does not preserve coalitions.

It accelerates their internal decay.

Closing Position

The Iliad is not a story of an alliance defeated by Troy.

It is a record of an alliance undermined by **its own assumptions**.

The Greeks do not lose because they lack strength.
 They nearly lose because they misunderstand alignment.

This chapter establishes the central warning of Part III:

> **Coalitions do not fail when enemies attack.**
> **They fail when alignment is assumed instead of maintained.**

Every chapter that follows will examine a different fracture point—but all rest on this foundation:

Coalitions are fragile by default.

And the moment you forget that,
 they begin to fall apart—
  quietly, internally, and inevitably.

Chapter 11

Humiliation as a Breaking Event

Core Reality

**Public disrespect fractures alignment.
Humiliation invites withdrawal or sabotage.
Apologies rarely reverse it.**

---

1. Why Humiliation Is Not "Just an Emotion"

Most systems treat humiliation as an internal experience.

A feeling.
A reaction.
A personal sensitivity.

The Iliad does not.

It treats humiliation as an **event**.

Something that happens *in public*, alters status, recalibrates hierarchy, and permanently changes how individuals relate to the system that exposed them.

This chapter formalizes the AWH position clearly:

> **Humiliation is not how someone feels.**
> **It is what the system does to someone in front of witnesses.**

Once humiliation occurs, alignment does not weaken gradually.

It breaks.

---

2. What Makes Humiliation Structurally Different from Insult

Insults can be ignored.
Disrespect can be contextualized.
Loss can be recovered.

Humiliation cannot.

Because humiliation has three defining properties:

1. **Public visibility**

2. **Status degradation**

3. **Inescapable meaning**

In *The Iliad*, Agamemnon does not merely offend Achilles.

He humiliates him by:

- Seizing his prize publicly

- Doing so through formal authority

- Establishing precedent

The injury is not emotional volatility.

It is **structural demotion**.

This distinction matters.

> **Humiliation changes how others are allowed to treat you.**

Once that change occurs, identity defense activates immediately.

---

3. Why Public Disrespect Fractures Alignment Instantly

Alignment depends on shared assumptions:

- That contribution is valued

- That status is stable

- That hierarchy is predictable

Humiliation destroys all three at once.

Achilles does not question whether the Greeks need him.
He questions whether remaining aligned is **self-annihilating**.

From that moment forward, cooperation becomes irrational.

This is the AWH diagnostic:

> **Alignment fails when participation validates your own diminishment.**

At that point, withdrawal is not emotional.
It is protective.

---

4. Humiliation Rewrites Incentives

Before humiliation:

- Cooperation produces benefit

- Participation reinforces identity

After humiliation:

- Cooperation legitimizes degradation

- Participation confirms weakness

This incentive reversal is immediate and irreversible unless publicly addressed.

Achilles' calculus changes in an instant.

The war's outcome no longer matters as much as **not consenting to erasure**.

This is why humiliation is so dangerous to coalitions:

It flips incentives without altering objectives.

The system still wants victory.
 The individual now wants distance.

---

5. Withdrawal: The First and Most Common Response

Humiliation rarely produces immediate rebellion.

It produces **withdrawal**.

Withdrawal is the safest response because it:

- Preserves dignity

- Avoids escalation

- Withholds value without confrontation

Achilles does not attack Agamemnon.
He does not defect.
He does not rally opposition.

He disengages.

This is not passivity.
It is **silent opposition**.

Systems misread withdrawal as temporary.
It is often permanent.

---

6. Sabotage as the Secondary Response

When withdrawal is impossible—or punished—humiliation produces sabotage.

Sabotage is not always deliberate.
It often manifests as:

- Reduced effort

- Missed opportunities

- Selective compliance

- Information withholding

The Iliad shows this indirectly.

Greek effectiveness collapses not because soldiers defect—but because the system has lost its keystone contributor.

This is the second AWH rule of humiliation:

> **If withdrawal is blocked, humiliation turns inward and destabilizes execution.**

---

7. Why Humiliation Is So Hard to Reverse

Systems believe time heals humiliation.

It does not.

Humiliation persists because:

- The audience remembers

- The precedent stands

- The hierarchy remains unchanged

Apologies fail because they do not alter the original signal.

Agamemnon apologizes.
 He offers gifts.
 He acknowledges excess.

Nothing changes.

Why?

Because the **public meaning** remains intact:

- He humiliated Achilles

- He retained authority

- He suffered no consequence

The humiliation is confirmed, not erased.

---

8. The False Promise of Apology

Apologies assume the problem is emotional.

Humiliation is structural.

An apology that does not:

- Reverse the status loss

- Acknowledge public wrongdoing publicly

- Recalibrate authority

is interpreted as **containment**, not repair.

This is why the AWH rule is uncompromising:

> **Apologies rarely reverse humiliation because they preserve the hierarchy that caused it.**

To reverse humiliation requires visible cost at the top.

Most systems will not pay it.

---

9. Why Humiliation Hardens Over Time

If humiliation is not repaired immediately, it hardens into identity.

The injured party stops seeking redress.
They stop negotiating.
They stop explaining.

They begin reorganizing their behavior **away from the system**.

Achilles' silence deepens.
His refusal becomes absolute.

Time does not soften this.
It clarifies it.

Every Greek death that follows reinforces Achilles' separation.

---

10. The Audience Effect: How Humiliation Spreads

Humiliation never affects only one person.

Witnesses update their expectations.

Greek warriors observe:

- Achilles humiliated

- Authority unchecked

- Excellence unprotected

They learn:

- Status is fragile

- Loyalty is unsafe

- Contribution does not guarantee security

This erodes alignment across the coalition.

Even those not humiliated begin disengaging psychologically.

This is why humiliation is contagious.

---

11. Why Systems Create Humiliation Accidentally

Most humiliations are not intentional.

They arise from:

- Authority asserting control

- Efficiency overriding symbolism

- Discipline applied without foresight

Agamemnon does not intend to fracture the coalition.
 He intends to preserve authority.

Humiliation is the **unintended byproduct of power exercised without regard for public meaning**.

This is why it recurs so frequently.

---

12. Humiliation vs. Discipline

Systems often justify humiliating acts as discipline.

This is a category error.

Discipline corrects behavior.
 Humiliation degrades identity.

Discipline can coexist with alignment.
 Humiliation cannot.

The Iliad demonstrates that punishment which alters public status produces resistance—not compliance.

---

13. Modern Systems, Same Breaking Event

Humiliation remains one of the fastest ways to destroy alignment in modern systems.

It appears when:

- Leaders are criticized publicly by allies

- Contributors are blamed in front of peers

- Credit is reassigned visibly

- Authority shames rather than corrects

The language is modern.
 The response is ancient.

Withdrawal follows.
Sabotage appears.
Apologies fail.

---

14. Strategic Implication (Without Prescription)

This framework does not offer conflict-resolution strategies.
It does not recommend apology protocols.
It does not propose reconciliation tactics.

It diagnoses reality.

If humiliation is a breaking event, then:

- Public disrespect must be treated as irreversible unless immediately addressed

- Silence after humiliation is not stability—it is exit

- Apologies that preserve hierarchy are confirmation, not repair

- Coalitions should treat humiliation as catastrophic risk

Ignoring these truths does not preserve authority.

It accelerates collapse.

Closing Position

The Iliad does not depict Achilles as volatile.

It depicts him as **structurally injured**.

Agamemnon does not merely offend him.
 He humiliates him.

From that moment forward, the coalition is broken—whether anyone admits it or not.

This is the final, non-negotiable truth of humiliation:

> **Once someone is publicly reduced,**
> **alignment is no longer assumed—it must be**
> **re-earned.**

And most systems discover this too late,
 after silence has replaced loyalty,
 after withdrawal has replaced cooperation,
 and after apology has become meaningless.

Humiliation is not an emotion to manage.

It is a breaking event to prevent.

Because once it happens,
 the system has already lost something it cannot replace.

Chapter 12

Unequal Burden, Unequal Cost

Core Reality

Disproportionate sacrifice breeds resentment.
Invisible contribution erodes trust.
Reward mismatch destabilizes unity.

---

1. The Quiet Mathematics That Breaks Coalitions

Coalitions rarely collapse over ideology.

They collapse over **accounting**.

Not financial accounting—but **burden accounting**:

- Who sacrifices

- Who decides

- Who benefits

- Who is protected

Every coalition runs a silent ledger.

People may not speak it aloud.
 They may not formalize it.
 But they track it relentlessly.

The Iliad demonstrates this truth repeatedly:

> **When the burden ledger and the reward ledger
> diverge, alignment fails—even if the objective
> remains unchanged.**

This chapter formalizes the AWH principle that underlies countless historical and modern collapses:

> **Unity depends less on shared goals than on
> perceived proportionality of cost and recognition.**

---

2. Why Unequal Burden Is Not Immediately Destabilizing

One of the most misunderstood aspects of coalition failure is timing.

Unequal burden does not cause instant revolt.

It causes **delayed erosion**.

People tolerate imbalance when:

- They believe it is temporary

- They believe it is acknowledged

- They believe it will be corrected

In *The Iliad*, Greek soldiers endure extraordinary sacrifice:

- Years away from home

- Constant combat

- High casualty rates

They accept this because they believe:

- Victory will justify the cost

- Leaders are sharing risk symbolically

- Honor distribution reflects sacrifice

The moment this belief weakens, resentment begins.

Not loudly.
 Not dramatically.

Silently.

3. Disproportionate Sacrifice Breeds Resentment—Not Rebellion

Resentment is not rebellion.

It is **pre-rebellion**.

It forms when individuals experience:

- Repeated sacrifice

- Without proportional recognition

- Under leaders insulated from consequence

This resentment rarely expresses itself directly.

Why?

Because rebellion is risky.
Because silence is safer.
Because endurance feels honorable—until it doesn't.

In *The Iliad*, resentment does not explode among the rank-and-file.

It accumulates.

Greek soldiers continue to fight after Achilles withdraws.
They obey commands.
They hold the line.

But something has changed.

They no longer believe the system is **fairly distributing cost**.

This belief matters more than morale slogans or shared enemies.

---

4. Invisible Contribution: The Fastest Way to Destroy Trust

Trust does not erode only when burden is unequal.

It erodes when **contribution is invisible**.

Invisible contribution occurs when:

- Effort is normalized

- Sacrifice is expected

- Risk is unacknowledged

- Loss is treated as inevitable

In *The Iliad*, unnamed soldiers die by the thousands.

Their deaths are recorded as fate.
As necessity.
As the cost of war.

They are not individualized.
They are not recognized.
They are not compensated symbolically.

Meanwhile, leadership disputes dominate attention.

This creates a devastating contrast:

Those who sacrifice most are seen least.

Trust cannot survive this condition.

---

5. Why Recognition Matters More Than Compensation

Systems often attempt to correct burden imbalance through material compensation.

More pay.
More reward.
More future promise.

This misunderstands the problem.

The issue is not payment.
It is **visibility**.

Recognition communicates:

- That sacrifice is noticed

- That cost is understood

- That loss has meaning

Without recognition, compensation feels transactional.
And transactional framing cheapens sacrifice.

Achilles understands this intuitively.

Greek soldiers feel it collectively.

This is the AWH diagnostic:

> **Invisible sacrifice does not feel heroic.**
> **It feels disposable.**

Once sacrifice feels disposable, trust collapses.

---

6. The Leader Insulation Problem

Coalitions tolerate unequal burden only if leaders appear to share risk.

In *The Iliad*, leaders are physically present in battle—but symbolically insulated.

Agamemnon's authority is never endangered by the losses his decisions produce.
His status remains intact.
His position is secure.

This insulation creates asymmetry:

- Leaders argue

- Warriors die

The problem is not hierarchy.
It is **cost insulation without symbolic reciprocity**.

When leaders absorb none of the moral or symbolic cost of failure, resentment accelerates.

---

7. Reward Mismatch as Coalition Poison

Reward mismatch occurs when:

- Those who sacrifice receive less recognition

- Those who decide receive more protection

- Outcomes reward position rather than contribution

This mismatch destabilizes unity faster than defeat.

Why?

Because it reframes participation as exploitation.

In *The Iliad*, Achilles' honor is stripped while others benefit from
his prior victories.
 Rank-and-file soldiers die while leadership retains prestige.

The coalition still fights Troy.

But internally, belief fractures.

This is the AWH principle made explicit:

> **People will endure loss for a cause.**
> **They will not endure loss for someone else's ego.**

---

8. Why Unequal Cost Is Often Denied by Systems

Systems resist acknowledging unequal burden because doing so
threatens legitimacy.

Admitting unequal cost requires admitting:

- That leadership decisions harm others disproportionately

- That hierarchy protects itself

- That sacrifice is not equally shared

It is easier to frame losses as:

- Necessary

- Inevitable

- Noble

This framing delays reckoning.
It does not prevent it.

---

9. How Unequal Burden Manifests Behaviorally

Unequal burden does not immediately produce defiance.

It produces subtle behavioral shifts:

- Reduced initiative

- Narrow compliance

- Emotional withdrawal

- Loss of discretionary effort

In *The Iliad*, this manifests as:

- Weaker battle cohesion

- Higher casualty rates

- Loss of confidence

- Dependence on a shrinking pool of heroes

The coalition becomes brittle.

Not because people stop showing up.
But because they stop **believing**.

---

10. The Illusion of Unity Under Pressure

External threat can temporarily mask burden imbalance.

Fear forces alignment.
Urgency suppresses dissent.

This creates the illusion of unity.

In *The Iliad*, intense Trojan pressure keeps the Greek coalition
operational even as resentment grows.

Leaders misinterpret this as cohesion.

It is not.

It is constraint.

When pressure fluctuates, suppressed resentment surfaces—stronger than before.

---

11. Unequal Burden and Moral Injury

Unequal burden produces moral injury when individuals realize:

- Their suffering is avoidable

- Their loss serves internal disputes

- Their sacrifice is instrumental, not respected

This realization is devastating.

It does not create rage.
It creates **detachment**.

Detached participants do not revolt.
They disengage.

And disengaged coalitions do not survive prolonged pressure.

---

12. Why Systems Detect Collapse Too Late

Systems monitor performance metrics.

They do not monitor **belief metrics**.

As long as:

- Orders are followed

- Battles are fought

- Work is done

leaders assume unity persists.

By the time performance collapses, belief is already gone.

This is why coalition failure often appears sudden.

It is not.

It is deferred.

---

13. The Trojan Parallel: Same Ledger, Same Failure

This dynamic is not unique to the Greeks.

Trojan allies also bear unequal burden:

- Cities destroyed

- Lives lost

- Leaders insulated

As hope fades, commitment weakens.

Coalitions on both sides suffer from the same accounting failure.

This framework is not moral.

It is structural.

---

14. Modern Coalitions, Same Arithmetic

The arithmetic of unequal burden persists unchanged:

- Employees burn out while executives are rewarded

- Soldiers carry trauma while policymakers remain insulated

- Activists sacrifice while leaders gain visibility

- Creators labor while platforms profit

In every case:

- Contribution becomes invisible

- Burden becomes normalized

- Reward skews upward

Unity erodes.

---

15. Strategic Implication (Without Prescription)

This framework does not offer compensation models.
It does not propose incentive structures.
It does not recommend equity formulas.

It diagnoses reality.

If unequal burden destabilizes unity, then:

- Sacrifice must be made visible

- Recognition must track contribution

- Leaders cannot remain symbolically insulated

- Silence must be read as resentment

Ignoring these truths does not preserve coalitions.

It guarantees their decay.

Closing Position

The Iliad is not only a story of heroes and gods.

It is a ledger of **who paid**.

It records:

- Who sacrificed

- Who decided

- Who benefited

- Who was forgotten

Coalitions do not fail because sacrifice is high.

They fail because sacrifice is **uneven and unacknowledged**.

This chapter leaves behind a final, unavoidable truth:

Unity cannot survive when cost and recognition diverge.

Not because people are weak.
 Not because commitment fades.
 But because no collective can endure once participation feels indistinguishable from exploitation.

And once that realization spreads,
 the coalition may still stand—
 but it will no longer hold.

Chapter 13

Withdrawal as Strategic Collapse

Core Realities

**Silent disengagement precedes open conflict.
Non-participation is a warning signal.
Coalitions often die quietly.**

---

1. The Collapse That No One Sees

Most systems train for conflict.

They watch for:

- Mutiny

- Defection

- Sabotage

- Open dissent

They prepare contingency plans for visible threats.

What they do not train for is **absence**.

Withdrawal does not announce itself.
 It does not demand attention.
 It does not violate rules.

And because of that, it is the most lethal form of collapse.

This chapter establishes the AWH position unequivocally:

> **Systems do not fail when people fight them.**
> **They fail when people stop participating in them.**

The Iliad is explicit on this point.

The Greek coalition is not undone by rebellion.
 It is nearly destroyed by **one man stepping aside**.

---

2. Why Withdrawal Is Strategically Superior to Revolt

Revolt is expensive.

It:

- Clarifies sides

- Invites punishment

- Forces confrontation

- Burns bridges

Withdrawal does none of these.

Withdrawal:

- Preserves legitimacy

- Avoids retaliation

- Maintains dignity

- Maximizes systemic strain

Achilles does not attack Agamemnon.
He does not undermine command openly.
He does not defect to Troy.

He withdraws.

This is not emotional avoidance.
It is **strategic non-participation**.

The framework formalizes this rule:

> **When exit is costly and compliance is degrading,
> withdrawal becomes the optimal response.**

3. Silent Disengagement Comes First

Open conflict is rarely the beginning.

It is the end.

Before rebellion, there is:

- Silence

- Reduced initiative

- Narrow compliance

- Emotional distance

In *The Iliad*, Achilles' withdrawal is preceded by a change in posture.

He stops arguing.
He stops persuading.
He stops engaging.

This is the first and most critical warning sign.

> **When high-leverage actors stop speaking,
> the system is already in decline.**

Coalitions misinterpret silence as cooling off.

It is not.

It is exit without departure.

---

4. Why Non-Participation Is a Warning Signal, Not Apathy

Systems often dismiss withdrawal as laziness, sulking, or immaturity.

This is a catastrophic misread.

Withdrawal requires discipline.

It requires:

- Restraint

- Risk tolerance

- Long-term thinking

Achilles' non-participation costs Greek lives.
 It costs him reputation.
 It costs him immediate influence.

He accepts those costs because participation would validate humiliation and erasure.

This is the AWH diagnostic:

---

5. Withdrawal Preserves Moral High Ground

One reason withdrawal is so powerful is that it avoids moral exposure.

Rebellion can be framed as betrayal.
Sabotage can be condemned.
Defiance can be punished.

Withdrawal offers no such handle.

Achilles does not violate rules.
He does not attack allies.
He does not undermine objectives directly.

He simply withholds what only he can provide.

The system has no clean response.

Punishing withdrawal escalates fracture.
Ignoring it accelerates loss.

This is why withdrawal is so destabilizing.

---

6. The Illusion of Stability During Withdrawal

Withdrawal does not immediately collapse systems.

That is why it is so dangerous.

After Achilles withdraws:

- The Greek army still exists

- Command still functions

- Battles are still fought

From the outside, the system appears intact.

Leaders interpret this as resilience.

It is not.

It is **momentum masking decay**.

This produces a false sense of security:

> **As long as the structure stands,**
> **leaders assume alignment remains.**

By the time outcomes deteriorate, the cause is already past.

7. Withdrawal Redistributes Cost Invisibly

When a critical contributor withdraws, the system does not halt.

It compensates.

Others take on more risk.
Others work harder.
Others die.

The cost of withdrawal is rarely borne by the withdrawer alone.

In *The Iliad*, Greek soldiers absorb the full cost of Achilles' absence.

This creates secondary fractures:

- Resentment among those still participating

- Moral injury from avoidable loss

- Erosion of belief in leadership

Withdrawal thus cascades.

It is not a single absence.
It is a **structural shockwave**.

8. Why Coalitions Misinterpret Withdrawal as Temporary

Systems assume withdrawal is a phase.

They believe:

- Time will cool emotions

- Incentives will restore participation

- Pressure will force return

This assumption is almost always wrong.

Withdrawal hardens over time.

Why?

Because each moment of absence:

- Reinforces separation

- Normalizes non-participation

- Confirms identity outside the system

Achilles' withdrawal becomes identity-defining.

He is no longer "a Greek warrior temporarily angry."
He is something else.

This is the AWH rule systems refuse to learn:

> **The longer withdrawal persists,**
> **the less likely reintegration becomes.**

---

9. The Difference Between Burnout and Withdrawal

Not all disengagement is strategic.

Burnout is exhaustion.
Withdrawal is decision.

Burnout seeks relief.
Withdrawal seeks preservation.

In *The Iliad*, Achilles is not burned out.

He is resolute.

He maintains discipline.
He refuses gifts.
He sustains separation.

Confusing burnout with withdrawal leads systems to offer rest
when the issue is legitimacy.

This guarantees failure.

---

10. Withdrawal vs. Sabotage

When withdrawal is blocked, sabotage emerges.

If individuals cannot step aside without punishment, they begin disengaging internally.

This manifests as:

- Minimal compliance

- Reduced vigilance

- Withheld information

- Strategic incompetence

Sabotage is withdrawal turned inward.

The Iliad does not dwell on this explicitly—but the outcome is visible.

Without Achilles, Greek effectiveness collapses.

Not because soldiers defect.
But because the system has lost its center of gravity.

---

11. Why Coalitions Die Quietly

Coalitions rarely collapse in dramatic confrontation.

They erode through:

- Absence

- Silence

- Reduced belief

- Normalized disengagement

By the time rebellion appears, the coalition is already hollow.

This is why leaders are shocked when failure comes.

They were watching for noise.

The collapse happened in silence.

---

12. The Audience Effect of Withdrawal

Withdrawal is not private.

Others notice.

They observe:

- Who is missing

- Who is silent

- Who is no longer investing

They update their own behavior accordingly.

This produces a cascade.

Once one high-status contributor withdraws, others reassess their participation.

This is how coalitions unravel without anyone explicitly choosing collapse.

---

13. Modern Systems, Same Pattern

Withdrawal remains the dominant mode of failure in modern systems:

- Employees disengage long before they resign

- Partners go silent before exiting

- Allies reduce support before defecting

- Citizens withdraw belief before revolt

Leadership notices only when outcomes collapse.

By then, the exit already occurred.

---

14. Strategic Implication (Without Prescription)

This framework does not recommend forcing engagement.
It does not propose loyalty campaigns.
It does not suggest monitoring participation more aggressively.

It diagnoses reality.

If withdrawal is strategic collapse, then:

- Silence must be treated as signal

- Non-participation must be examined, not dismissed

- Continued structure must not be mistaken for alignment

- Absence must be understood as decision

Ignoring these truths does not preserve coalitions.

It blinds them.

Closing Position

The Iliad does not show the Greek coalition destroyed by revolt.

It shows it **bled nearly to death by absence**.

Achilles does not betray the Greeks.
He steps aside.

And in doing so, he reveals the final, uncomfortable truth of coalition failure:

> **Systems do not fall when people oppose them.**
> **They fall when people stop believing participation**
> **is worth the cost.**

By the time opposition becomes visible, the coalition is already gone.

Withdrawal is not the end of collapse.

It is the moment collapse begins—
quietly, invisibly, and too late to reverse.

PART IV

FAILURE MODES OF LEADERSHIP

How Leaders Accelerate Collapse Unintentionally

Chapter 14

Public Assertion of Authority

Core Realities

Public dominance invites resistance.
Authority asserted loudly is already weakening.
Force replaces legitimacy when pride is injured.

---

1. The Moment Leaders Reach for Volume

Leadership failure rarely begins with malice.

It begins with **anxiety**.

Specifically, the anxiety that authority is slipping.

At that moment, many leaders reach for the same tool:

Public assertion of authority.

They speak louder.
They assert rank.
They remind others who decides.
They invoke rules, hierarchy, and consequence—often in front of an audience.

From the leader's perspective, this feels corrective.
From the system's perspective, it feels stabilizing.

From the human perspective, it is a warning flare.

This chapter establishes the AWH position clearly:

**Authority asserted publicly is rarely preventative.
It is almost always reactive.**

And reaction is the beginning of collapse.

---

2. Authority vs. Legitimacy: The Foundational Distinction

Leadership systems consistently conflate two concepts:

- **Authority**: the right to command

- **Legitimacy**: the willingness of others to comply

Authority can exist without legitimacy.
Legitimacy cannot exist without trust.

Public assertion of authority is often an attempt to compensate for declining legitimacy.

In *The Iliad*, Agamemnon possesses unquestioned authority.
He is the king of kings.
No one disputes his formal right to command.

What he lacks—fatally—is legitimacy in the eyes of Achilles and, by extension, the coalition.

When legitimacy erodes, authority becomes louder.

Not stronger.
Louder.

This is the first diagnostic rule of this chapter:

> **When authority must be declared, it is already contested.**

3. Why Leaders Assert Authority Publicly

Public assertion is chosen for three reasons:

1. **Visibility** – Leaders believe public displays deter dissent

2. **Speed** – Public dominance seems faster than negotiation

3. **Fear Management** – It reassures the leader more than the system

In *The Iliad*, Agamemnon's seizure of Briseis is not a private correction.

It is a **public act**.

Why?

Because Agamemnon is not merely addressing Achilles.
He is addressing the audience.

He is signaling:

- I am in control

- I cannot be challenged

- Hierarchy is intact

This signal is not neutral.

It injures pride.
It destabilizes legitimacy.
It escalates resistance.

---

4. Public Dominance Invites Resistance

Resistance is not always loud.

It is often silent.

Public dominance creates a dilemma for those beneath it:

- Submit publicly and accept diminishment

- Resist publicly and risk punishment

- Withdraw privately and preserve identity

The third option is usually chosen.

Achilles does not argue endlessly.
He does not stage rebellion.
He does not challenge Agamemnon's crown.

He withdraws.

This is the predictable outcome of public authority assertion:

When authority humiliates publicly, resistance reorganizes privately.

Leaders mistake the absence of confrontation for compliance.

It is not.

It is disengagement.

---

5. Why Loud Authority Signals Weakness

Strong authority is quiet.

It does not need announcement.
It does not require spectacle.
It does not depend on audience reaction.

When authority becomes performative, it signals internal doubt.

This is not psychological speculation.
It is structural.

Authority that rests on legitimacy:

- Expects compliance

- Does not need demonstration

- Absorbs disagreement

Authority that has lost legitimacy:

- Demands compliance

- Requires public reinforcement

- Punishes dissent

In *The Iliad*, Agamemnon's authority survives structurally.
His legitimacy collapses functionally.

This creates the illusion of strength—and the reality of fragility.

---

6. Public Assertion as a Status Weapon

Public authority assertions are rarely about order.

They are about **status repair**.

Agamemnon is injured when Achilles challenges him verbally.

The challenge occurs in front of the assembly.
The injury is public.

Agamemnon responds with a public act of dominance.

This is not governance.
It is **status warfare**.

The AWH diagnostic here is precise:

> **When leaders use authority to heal pride,**
> **they sacrifice legitimacy to restore self-image.**

The system pays the price.

---

7. Force Replaces Legitimacy When Pride Is Injured

Once pride is injured, leaders reinterpret dissent as threat.

They escalate from persuasion to command.
From explanation to decree.
From leadership to enforcement.

This shift is subtle but catastrophic.

Force does not mean violence.
It means **compulsion without consent**.

In *The Iliad*, Agamemnon does not strike Achilles.
He compels him.

The result is not obedience.
It is withdrawal.

This is the paradox leaders refuse to accept:

**The more authority relies on force,
the less authority it actually possesses.**

---

8. Why Public Assertion Fails to Produce Compliance

Public assertion fails because it misunderstands human alignment.

People do not align with authority.
They align with **meaning**.

Public dominance:

- Degrades meaning

- Threatens identity

- Signals instability

It forces people to choose between compliance and dignity.

Dignity usually wins—quietly.

Achilles' choice is not emotional.
It is strategic self-preservation.

9. The Audience Effect: Authority Is Never Asserted in Isolation

Public authority assertions are never contained.

The audience watches.

Greek warriors observe:

- Achilles humiliated

- Authority unchecked

- Excellence overridden

They update their beliefs.

Even those who remain compliant reassess loyalty.

This produces a secondary collapse:

- Reduced trust

- Narrowed compliance

- Loss of discretionary effort

The leader believes control has been restored.

The coalition has begun to hollow out.

---

10. Why Leaders Misread Silence After Assertion

After asserting authority, leaders often encounter silence.

They interpret this as success.

The meeting ends.
 Orders are followed.
 No one openly resists.

This is the most dangerous moment.

Silence after humiliation is not agreement.
 It is **exit preparation**.

Achilles' silence is absolute.

By the time the Greeks realize what it means, they are bleeding.

---

11. The Escalation Trap

Once public authority is asserted, leaders become trapped.

If they soften, they appear weak.
 If they double down, they deepen resistance.

This produces escalation without resolution.

Each assertion:

- Raises stakes

- Narrows options

- Increases cost

Agamemnon cannot reverse course without symbolic loss. Achilles cannot return without self-annihilation.

The system locks.

This is the AWH principle:

> **Public dominance creates situations where no one can back down without collapse.**

---

12. Authority vs. Alignment: The Hidden Tradeoff

Public authority assertions trade alignment for control.

Control feels safer.
 Alignment is actually safer.

Control requires enforcement.
Alignment produces cooperation.

In *The Iliad*, Agamemnon retains control.
He loses alignment.

The war continues.
The coalition weakens.
Losses mount.

This is the cost of confusing the two.

---

13. Modern Leadership, Same Failure Mode

This failure mode is not ancient.

It appears whenever leaders:

- Publicly shame subordinates

- Reassert rank in open forums

- Use authority to settle identity disputes

- Perform dominance to manage insecurity

Examples abound:

- CEOs humiliating executives publicly

- Political leaders silencing allies on stage

- Commanders dressing down officers in front of units

The intent is control.
The outcome is disengagement.

---

14. Why This Failure Mode Is So Seductive

Public assertion feels decisive.

It creates:

- Immediate compliance

- Visible hierarchy

- Emotional relief for the leader

The damage is delayed.

By the time consequences appear:

- The moment has passed

- The injury is normalized

- Withdrawal is entrenched

This delay is why leaders repeat the mistake.

---

15. Strategic Implication (Without Prescription)

This framework does not advise leaders to avoid authority.
It does not promote egalitarian fantasy.
It does not deny hierarchy.

It diagnoses reality.

If public assertion of authority accelerates collapse, then:

- Loud dominance should be treated as risk, not strength

- Silence after assertion should be treated as warning, not success

- Authority used to repair pride should be recognized as misapplied

- Control achieved at the cost of legitimacy is temporary

Ignoring these truths does not preserve leadership.

It converts authority into a blunt instrument that shatters the system it seeks to hold together.

Closing Position

The Iliad does not show Agamemnon losing his crown.

It shows him losing his coalition.

And he loses it not by weakness—but by **overassertion**.

This chapter leaves behind a final, uncomfortable truth:

> **When leaders assert authority publicly,**
> **it is rarely because they are strong.**
> **It is because they feel strength slipping.**

And every time authority replaces legitimacy,
the system takes one more step toward collapse—
quietly, structurally, and beyond the reach of command.

Chapter 15

Emotional Decision Contagion

Core Realities

Leader emotion spreads through systems.
Rage, fear, and grief propagate.
Discipline collapses without visible restraint.

---

1. The Myth of Contained Emotion in Leadership

Modern leadership culture promotes a comforting fiction:

That emotion is internal, private, and separable from decision-making.

This fiction collapses instantly under pressure.

In real systems—especially hierarchical ones—leader emotion is not contained.
It is **broadcast**.

Not always through words.
Not always through policy.
But through tone, posture, pacing, escalation, and tolerance.

The Iliad does not treat emotion as background color.

It treats emotion as **a vector**—a force that moves through the system and reshapes behavior at every level.

This chapter establishes a core AWH truth:

> **Emotion is not an individual experience in leadership contexts.**
> **It is a systemic condition.**

---

2. What Emotional Decision Contagion Actually Is

Emotional decision contagion is not "people copying feelings."

It is **decision logic being rewritten by observed emotional states**.

When a leader is calm:

- Decisions are slower

- Constraints are respected

- Proportionality matters

When a leader is enraged:

- Speed replaces deliberation

- Excess becomes acceptable

- Boundaries dissolve

Subordinates do not need instructions.

They adjust automatically.

This is the danger.

> **Emotion spreads not by persuasion, but by permission.**

---

3. Achilles as the Epicenter of Contagion

Achilles' emotional state does not remain his own.

His rage infects the battlefield.
His grief reshapes the war.
His loss of restraint becomes the system's loss of restraint.

After Patroclus' death, Achilles does not issue new doctrines.

He fights.

And everyone adapts to what they see.

> *"Then Achilles went forth, like inhuman fire."*

This is not metaphor.

It is a description of **emotional amplification**.

Once Achilles abandons restraint, restraint becomes optional for everyone else.

---

4. Why Leader Emotion Carries Structural Authority

Emotion at the top carries weight because leaders define:

- What is acceptable

- What is urgent

- What is forgivable

- What is excessive

When a leader rages, rage becomes legitimate.
 When a leader panics, panic becomes rational.
 When a leader grieves publicly, grief becomes the organizing logic.

No memo is required.

This is the AWH diagnostic:

> **Leaders do not need to command emotion.**
> **They authorize it by displaying it.**

---

5. Rage as Accelerant

Rage is the fastest-moving emotional contagion.

Why?

Because rage:

- Simplifies decisions

- Narrows options

- Justifies destruction

In *The Iliad*, Achilles' rage turns the battlefield into a furnace.

He stops taking prisoners.
He stops observing ritual limits.
He stops distinguishing necessity from excess.

Others follow.

Not because they are told to.
Because **restraint has been revoked at the top**.

---

6. Fear as Silent Contagion

Fear spreads differently.

It does not explode.
It contracts.

When leaders display fear:

- Risk tolerance collapses

- Initiative disappears

- Decision-making becomes defensive

Fear produces over-compliance and under-thinking.

In the Greek camp, fear spreads when Achilles withdraws and later when Trojan pressure intensifies.

Leaders overcorrect.
Warriors hesitate.
Mistakes multiply.

Fear does not shout.
It tightens.

---

7. Grief as System Rewriter

Grief is the most destabilizing emotional contagion because it
redefines purpose.

When leaders grieve openly and act from that grief:

- Long-term goals dissolve

- Symbolic actions dominate

- Sacrifice becomes unbounded

Achilles' grief does not just motivate vengeance.

It reorients the entire system toward **emotional resolution**, not
strategic outcome.

This is the AWH insight:

> **Grief does not coexist with optimization.**
> **It replaces it.**

8. Why Discipline Requires Visible Restraint

Discipline is not maintained through rules alone.

It is maintained through **modeled behavior**.

When leaders restrain themselves:

- Others hold back

- Boundaries remain credible

- Escalation is delayed

When leaders lose restraint:

- Discipline collapses without instruction

In *The Iliad*, Achilles' loss of restraint authorizes:

- Excess violence

- Disregard for norms

- Brutalization of combat

No council votes.
No orders are given.

The system adapts instantly.

---

9. The Collapse of Proportionality

Proportionality is the first casualty of emotional contagion.

Under rage, everything feels justified.
Under fear, everything feels urgent.
Under grief, nothing feels excessive.

Achilles drags Hector's body not because it is useful—but because restraint no longer exists.

> *"I would not care to let you lie unburied, though they offered me ten times your weight in ransom."*

This is not cruelty as personality.

It is discipline collapse as system condition.

---

10. Why Emotional Contagion Is So Often Misdiagnosed

Systems misdiagnose emotional contagion because:

- Results may temporarily improve

- Speed increases

- Compliance appears strong

This creates the illusion of effectiveness.

In *The Iliad*, Achilles' return reverses battlefield momentum.

Leaders mistake this for success.

It is not.

It is **short-term output purchased with long-term collapse**.

---

11. Contagion Without Intent

The most dangerous aspect of emotional contagion is that it does not require intent.

Achilles does not intend to destabilize norms.
 Agamemnon does not intend to spread fear.
 Leaders rarely intend emotional spillover.

It happens anyway.

This is why emotional discipline is not a personal virtue.

It is a **systemic requirement**.

12. The Audience Effect Revisited

Every emotional display by a leader is observed.

Not just by direct subordinates—but by:

- Peers

- Rivals

- Bystanders

They update their behavior accordingly.

This is why emotional outbursts are never isolated incidents.

They are **broadcast events**.

---

13. Modern Systems, Same Contagion

Emotional decision contagion is not ancient.

It appears whenever:

- Executives rage in meetings

- Political leaders panic publicly

- Commanders act from grief

- Founders oscillate emotionally

Organizations adapt.

Not to the strategy—but to the emotion.

Culture becomes reactive.
Discipline erodes.
Decision quality collapses.

---

14. Why Leaders Underestimate Their Emotional Reach

Leaders often believe:

- "I'm just venting."

- "They know I don't mean it."

- "This is personal."

It is never personal.

Once you lead, emotion becomes **infrastructure**.

Your mood becomes environment.
Your restraint becomes policy.
Your excess becomes permission.

---

15. Strategic Implication (Without Prescription)

This framework does not advise emotional suppression.
It does not recommend performative calm.
It does not deny humanity.

It diagnoses reality.

If emotional decision contagion exists, then:

- Leader emotion must be treated as system input

- Loss of restraint must be recognized as structural risk

- Short-term gains from emotional escalation must be distrusted

- Discipline must be visibly modeled, not verbally enforced

Ignoring these truths does not make systems resilient.

It makes them reactive.

Closing Position

The Iliad does not portray emotional leaders as weak.

It portrays them as **dangerously influential**.

Achilles' rage does not stay inside him.
 It becomes the war.

This chapter closes with the final, unavoidable truth of leadership emotion:

> **When leaders lose emotional restraint,**
> **they do not just make bad decisions.**
> **They teach everyone else to do the same.**

And once discipline collapses at the top,
 no amount of rules, hierarchy, or authority
 can restore it in time to prevent collapse.

Emotion spreads faster than orders.

And systems always follow the strongest signal they receive.

Chapter 16

Misreading Silence

Core Realities

Silence is interpreted as agreement.
Silence often signals injury.
Silence precedes fracture.

---

1. The Most Expensive Misinterpretation in Leadership

Among all leadership errors, few are as consistently catastrophic as this one:

Interpreting silence as consent.

Silence feels reassuring.
It lowers tension.
It ends meetings.
It restores order—temporarily.

For leaders under pressure, silence reads as resolution.

In reality, silence is often **the moment alignment ends**.

The Iliad demonstrates this repeatedly.
Not through speeches.
Not through rebellion.
But through absence, quiet, and refusal to engage.

This chapter formalizes a core AWH truth:

> **Silence is not neutrality.**
> **Silence is a decision state.**

And by the time silence appears, the system is already late.

---

2. Why Systems Prefer Silence

Silence is comforting.

It offers leaders:

- The illusion of closure

- The appearance of unity

- The absence of confrontation

Silence allows authority to proceed without resistance.

This is why systems **reward silence unintentionally**.

Meetings end faster.
Orders move smoothly.
Decisions appear final.

But silence does not mean alignment.

It means **non-engagement**.

And non-engagement is the first irreversible step toward collapse.

---

3. Silence Is Not Passive — It Is Strategic

Silence requires discipline.

It is chosen when:

- Speaking would legitimize harm

- Protest would escalate punishment

- Participation would erode identity

Achilles does not continue arguing with Agamemnon.

He stops speaking.

This is not fatigue.
It is **withdrawal with intent**.

The AWH diagnostic is clear:

> **People go silent when speech no longer protects them.**

Silence is not lack of opinion.
It is lack of safety—or lack of perceived value in participation.

---

4. Silence as a Signal of Injury

In healthy systems, injury produces dialogue.

In unhealthy systems, injury produces silence.

Why?

Because speaking after injury often:

- Confirms vulnerability

- Invites further harm

- Produces no repair

Achilles speaks once—forcefully.
He is humiliated publicly.
He then becomes silent.

This sequence matters.

Silence does not appear randomly.
 It follows **failed expression**.

This is the rule leaders miss:

> **Silence usually follows the moment someone realizes speaking no longer works.**

---

5. The Illusion of Resolution

After confrontation, silence feels like peace.

Leaders believe:

- "They've accepted it."

- "They've cooled off."

- "The issue is settled."

In *The Iliad*, Agamemnon interprets Achilles' silence as submission.

He is wrong.

The issue is not settled.
 It is **sealed**.

Silence closes the door on negotiation.
 Not because agreement was reached—but because participation was withdrawn.

---

6. Why Silence Precedes Fracture

Fracture is noisy.
 Silence is quiet.

Because fracture requires:

- Energy

- Exposure

- Risk

Silence avoids all three.

Before coalitions fracture:

- High-status actors stop contributing

- Low-status actors disengage emotionally

- Initiative collapses

- Feedback loops die

This is what happens in the Greek camp.

No mutiny.
 No revolt.
 No dramatic confrontation.

Just **deterioration**.

This is the AWH principle this chapter centers:

> **Fracture is preceded by silence the way collapse
> is preceded by cracks.**

---

7. Silence vs. Agreement: The Category Error

Agreement produces participation.
 Silence produces compliance at best—and often not even that.

Agreement is active.
 Silence is withholding.

Leaders conflate the two because both are quiet.

But they produce radically different futures.

Agreement sustains systems.
 Silence drains them.

Achilles' silence costs the Greeks their most decisive advantage.

And the system never formally recognizes the loss until it is
bleeding.

---

8. The Audience Effect of Silence

Silence is observed.

Others notice who stops speaking.
Who stops volunteering.
Who stops investing.

They update their own behavior accordingly.

Silence spreads.

This produces a cascading effect:

- One person disengages

- Others reduce effort

- Trust erodes

- Initiative collapses

No one announces departure.
The coalition simply hollows out.

---

9. Why Leaders Rarely Probe Silence

Silence is dangerous to question.

If leaders probe silence, they risk:

- Reopening conflict

- Discovering injury

- Confronting legitimacy loss

It is safer to accept quiet as success.

This avoidance accelerates collapse.

The AWH rule here is blunt:

Unquestioned silence is mismanagement.

Silence requires interpretation—not relief.

---

10. Silence as Identity Preservation

Silence preserves dignity.

When systems humiliate publicly or dismiss concerns, silence becomes the only remaining form of self-respect.

Achilles' silence allows him to:

- Avoid further degradation

- Maintain internal coherence

- Refuse symbolic submission

Speaking again would mean conceding meaning.

This is why silence hardens over time.

It becomes identity.

---

11. Silence Is Not Always Conscious — But It Is Always Informative

Not all silence is calculated.

Some silence is exhaustion.
 Some is fear.
 Some is learned helplessness.

But all silence carries information.

It says:

- "This system is unsafe."

- "This system does not listen."

- "This system no longer deserves me."

Ignoring that message does not make it disappear.

It ensures it will surface later—louder and more destructive.

---

12. Silence and the Redistribution of Cost

When people go silent, systems do not stop.

They compensate.

Others carry more weight.
Others absorb more risk.
Others burn out.

Silence thus redistributes cost invisibly.

By the time leadership notices performance collapse, the silent exit has already occurred.

---

13. Modern Systems, Same Failure

Silence remains the primary early-warning signal of collapse in modern systems:

- Employees disengage long before quitting

- Partners stop contributing before leaving

- Allies reduce communication before defecting

- Citizens withdraw belief before revolting

Leaders are shocked when outcomes fail.

They should not be.

The silence was the message.

---

14. Why Silence Is More Dangerous Than Dissent

Dissent can be engaged.
Debate can be managed.
Conflict can be negotiated.

Silence cannot.

Silence offers no leverage.
No feedback.
No opportunity for repair.

Once silence appears, the system is negotiating with an absence.

And absences do not compromise.

---

15. Strategic Implication (Without Prescription)

This framework does not advise leaders to force speech.
It does not recommend surveillance of engagement.
It does not propose participation mandates.

It diagnoses reality.

If silence signals injury and precedes fracture, then:

- Quiet should be treated as risk, not success

- Loss of voice should be investigated, not ignored

- Continued structure should not be mistaken for belief

- Silence after conflict should trigger alarm, not relief

Ignoring these truths does not preserve unity.

It guarantees surprise.

Closing Position

The Iliad does not depict collapse beginning with rebellion.

It begins with **silence**.

Achilles stops speaking.
Others stop believing.
The coalition bleeds.

This chapter leaves behind one final, unforgiving truth:

**Systems do not fail when people argue.
They fail when people stop speaking.**

And by the time silence feels comfortable,
the fracture has already begun.

Chapter 17

Moral Injury

Core Realities

**Violating personal or collective codes fractures identity.
Injury persists even after victory.
Moral cost compounds long-term damage.**

---

1. Why Moral Injury Is the Failure No System Plans For

Systems plan for loss.
They plan for attrition.
They plan for defeat.

They do **not** plan for **moral injury**.

Because moral injury does not announce itself.
It does not halt operations.
It does not always reduce output.

In fact, moral injury often coexists with *success*.

This is what makes it so dangerous.

The Iliad is filled with victory—battlefield dominance, heroic feats, enemy destruction.

It is also saturated with moral injury.

And the poem is unambiguous about one thing:

> **Winning does not heal moral damage.**
> **It often deepens it.**

This chapter formalizes the AWH position:

> **Moral injury is what remains when people survive actions their identity cannot justify.**

---

2. What Moral Injury Actually Is (And Is Not)

Moral injury is frequently confused with:

- Guilt

- Shame

- Trauma

- Regret

It is none of these.

Guilt says: *I did something wrong.*
Shame says: *I am something wrong.*
Trauma says: *Something overwhelming happened to me.*

Moral injury says something far more destabilizing:

> *I participated in actions that violated the code that
> makes me who I am.*

This is not about emotion.
It is about **identity coherence**.

In *The Iliad*, warriors are not merely afraid or traumatized.

They are forced into actions that:

- Violate ritual norms

- Break codes of honor

- Degrade enemies beyond accepted limits

- Sacrifice innocents for status disputes

Each violation leaves residue.

Not visible.
Not loud.

But permanent.

3. Codes Matter Because They Anchor Identity

Every collective system operates atop explicit or implicit codes:

- Honor

- Duty

- Justice

- Reciprocity

- Proportionality

These codes do not exist to make people moral.

They exist to make action **livable**.

Codes tell participants:

- *Why this is worth doing*

- *What will not be asked of me*

- *Where the line is*

Moral injury occurs when:

- The line is crossed

- The crossing is justified by authority

- The cost is borne by the individual

This is why moral injury is so corrosive.

It does not just hurt.
It **unanchors meaning**.

---

4. Achilles After Hector: The Moment Injury Becomes Visible

The most explicit depiction of moral injury in *The Iliad* occurs **after** Achilles' greatest victory.

Hector is dead.
The enemy's champion is defeated.
The war tilts decisively.

And Achilles does something that cannot be undone.

> *"Three times he dragged him round the well-built city
> of Priam."*

This act violates every warrior code the poem has established.

It is excessive.
It is symbolic.
It is irreversible.

Achilles wins—and is morally injured in the process.

This matters.

Because from this point on, Achilles is no longer whole—even though he is triumphant.

---

5. Why Moral Injury Persists After Victory

Victory resolves objectives.
Moral injury concerns **self-recognition**.

You can win and still be unable to live with what winning required.

In *The Iliad*, victory does not restore:

- Peace

- Coherence

- Closure

Instead, it leaves survivors carrying acts they cannot integrate.

This produces a critical AWH diagnostic:

**Moral injury is not erased by success.
It is often created by it.**

Systems that treat victory as closure misunderstand this
completely.

---

6. The Compounding Nature of Moral Injury

Moral injury compounds.

Not linearly.
 Exponentially.

Each unaddressed violation:

- Lowers resistance to the next

- Normalizes excess

- Rewrites what is "acceptable"

This is why restraint collapses over time.

Once Hector's body is desecrated, other boundaries feel less real.
 Once mercy is denied, cruelty becomes easier.

Once codes are broken with justification, they stop functioning as anchors.

This is not moral decay.
It is **adaptive numbing**.

And it spreads.

---

7. Moral Injury as a Systemic Force

Moral injury is often treated as an individual burden.

In reality, it is systemic.

When many individuals carry unresolved moral injury:

- Trust collapses

- Cynicism replaces belief

- Loyalty becomes transactional

- Identity detaches from mission

In *The Iliad*, warriors continue to fight—but belief erodes.

They perform.
They comply.
They survive.

But the war becomes something else.

This is the AWH principle:

> **Systems can function long after their moral core has collapsed.**

They just do not survive intact.

---

8. Why Moral Injury Is So Hard to Name

Moral injury resists articulation.

Why?

Because naming it requires admitting:

- That authority asked too much

- That leaders crossed lines

- That sacrifice was unjustified

Most systems cannot tolerate this admission.

So moral injury goes unnamed.

It manifests instead as:

- Withdrawal

- Aggression

- Emotional numbness

- Hyper-control

- Loss of meaning

Leaders misdiagnose these as discipline problems.

They are not.

They are **moral fractures**.

---

9. The Difference Between Moral Injury and Disobedience

Moral injury does not produce immediate rebellion.

It produces **moral disengagement**.

People stop believing the system deserves their full self.

They still act.
They still perform.
But something essential is withheld.

This is why moral injury often precedes:

- Silence

- Withdrawal

- Burnout

- Ethical collapse

And why punishing these symptoms worsens the damage.

---

10. Why Authority Cannot Repair Moral Injury Alone

Authority can compel behavior.
It cannot restore moral coherence.

Orders cannot heal code violations.
Rewards cannot undo participation in injustice.
Silence cannot erase memory.

In *The Iliad*, no command repairs Achilles' injury.

Not even Priam's appeal restores Hector's dignity retroactively.

"Remember your own father, great godlike Achilles."

The appeal reaches Achilles—but it does not undo what has been done.

This is the tragedy.

---

11. Moral Injury and the Illusion of Clean Endings

Systems crave clean endings.

Wars end.
 Projects close.
 Objectives are met.

Moral injury ignores these boundaries.

It carries forward.

Veterans return.
 Leaders retire.
 Institutions persist.

The injury remains.

This is why moral injury is often discovered **after** the system declares success.

When:

- People disengage

- Meaning collapses

- Trust cannot be rebuilt

The cost arrives late.

---

12. Why Moral Injury Is Often Misread as Weakness

Systems misread moral injury as:

- Fragility

- Sensitivity

- Disloyalty

- Lack of resilience

This framing is catastrophic.

Because moral injury is not weakness.

It is evidence that a person's internal code was **strong enough to be broken**.

This is the AWH correction:

The people most affected by moral injury are often the most principled participants.

Losing them costs systems their ethical center.

---

13. Moral Injury at the Collective Level

Collectives develop moral injury too.

When groups participate in actions that violate shared values:

- Narratives fracture

- Identity destabilizes

- History becomes contested

The Iliad itself is a record of this struggle.

It does not celebrate the war.
It mourns what it required.

This is not nostalgia.
It is reckoning.

---

14. Modern Systems, Same Wound

Moral injury persists in modern systems wherever people are required to:

- Enforce policies they believe are unjust

- Harm others for institutional survival

- Sacrifice innocents for optics or power

- Remain silent about wrongdoing

Organizations may succeed.
Campaigns may win.
Objectives may be achieved.

The injury remains.

And it shapes everything that follows.

---

15. Strategic Implication (Without Prescription)

This framework does not offer healing protocols.
It does not prescribe reconciliation rituals.
It does not propose moral repair programs.

It diagnoses reality.

If moral injury compounds long-term damage, then:

- Victory cannot be treated as closure

- Performance cannot be mistaken for belief

- Silence cannot be assumed to mean resolution

- Systems must assume invisible cost after visible success

Ignoring these truths does not preserve strength.

It hollow outs systems from within.

Closing Position

The Iliad is not ultimately about who wins.

It is about what winning costs—and who carries that cost afterward.

Achilles survives.
 Troy falls.
 The war ends.

And something essential is lost.

This chapter closes with the most difficult truth in the framework:

**Moral injury is the price systems pay when they
demand actions that identities cannot survive.**

You may still win.
 You may still advance.
 You may still function.

But you will not emerge unchanged.

And if the injury is ignored,
 the system will carry it forward—
 into every future decision,
 every future coalition,
 every future collapse.

PART V

APPLICATION WITHOUT REPAIR

Why This Framework Diagnoses but Does Not Solve

Chapter 18

Leadership in Organizations

Core Realities

Performance can persist without recognition.
Public correction destroys dignity faster than failure.
High performers disengage quietly, not dramatically.

---

1. Why This Chapter Exists (and Why It Does Not Fix Anything)

Most leadership books end by offering remedies.

Frameworks that diagnose failure are expected to pivot toward:

- Best practices

- Action plans

- Cultural playbooks

- Tactical corrections

This framework refuses to do that.

Not because solutions are impossible—but because **most organizational collapse does not occur due to lack of knowledge**.

It occurs because leaders apply force where recognition is required, process where dignity is at stake, and metrics where meaning has already collapsed.

This chapter applies the framework to modern organizations precisely to show **why repair often fails**, even when leaders are competent, informed, and well-intentioned.

The Iliad is not ancient history here.

It is pattern.

2. Organizations Are Coalitions with Longer Memory

Modern organizations differ from armies only in tempo.

They are still:

- Coalitions of unequal incentives

- Hierarchies of rank vs status

- Systems that displace cost downward

- Structures that reward silence

What changes is visibility.

In organizations:

- Withdrawal is subtle

- Silence is normalized

- Disengagement is productive-looking

People do not stop working.
 They stop *belonging*.

This is why organizations often appear healthy right up until they are not.

3. Performance Without Recognition: The Illusion of Health

One of the most dangerous organizational conditions is this:

High performance with declining belief.

This is the Achilles condition.

In *The Iliad*, Greek forces continue to fight effectively even as alignment collapses. Losses mount, but operations continue.

In organizations, this looks like:

- Teams hitting targets

- Individuals delivering results

- Metrics remaining strong

Leaders interpret this as stability.

It is not.

It is **momentum without commitment**.

Performance can be coerced.
 Belief cannot.

4. Why Recognition Is Not a "Soft" Variable

Organizations routinely underestimate recognition because:

- It is not quantifiable

- It is symbolic

- It threatens hierarchy

Recognition is treated as optional.
A bonus.
A compliment.
A cultural nice-to-have.

This is a fundamental misread.

Recognition determines:

- Whether effort feels voluntary

- Whether sacrifice feels meaningful

- Whether contribution feels safe

Achilles does not withdraw because he is underpaid.

He withdraws because his contribution is publicly devalued.

Organizations repeat this mistake constantly.

---

5. Public Correction vs. Private Dignity

One of the fastest ways to trigger disengagement in organizations is **public correction**.

Public correction is often justified as:

- Transparency

- Accountability

- Cultural enforcement

In reality, it functions as humiliation.

In *The Iliad*, Agamemnon corrects Achilles publicly.
 The system fractures.

In organizations, public correction:

- Rewrites status

- Signals replaceability

- Invites withdrawal

Leaders often say:

> "It wasn't personal."

That is irrelevant.

Dignity is not personal.
It is **structural**.

---

6. Why Public Correction Feels Necessary to Leaders

Public correction serves leaders emotionally.

It:

- Reasserts control

- Signals authority

- Reassures observers

It also feels efficient.

Why address one person privately when you can "set an example"?

Because examples teach lessons beyond intent.

The lesson taught is rarely "do better."

It is usually:

- "You are not safe here."

- "Status is fragile."

- "Performance does not protect you."

Once that lesson is learned, engagement collapses.

---

7. The High Performer's Dilemma

High performers face a unique bind.

They:

- Carry disproportionate load

- Absorb systemic failure

- Become visible targets

And yet, they are expected to endure more with less acknowledgment.

This creates the Achilles paradox in organizations:

The more you contribute, the more you are exposed.

When recognition fails to track contribution, high performers do not rebel.

They withdraw.

They stop mentoring.
They stop proposing.
They stop warning.

They continue delivering—until they leave.

---

8. Why High Performers Disengage Quietly

High performers do not disengage loudly because:

- They have reputations to protect

- They understand consequences

- They do not need validation

Withdrawal is safer than protest.

This mirrors Achilles precisely.

He does not sabotage the Greeks.
He steps aside.

In organizations, this looks like:

- Reduced initiative

- Narrow scope compliance

- Strategic silence

Leaders often misread this as maturity.

It is not.

It is **exit in place**.

---

9. Silence as Organizational Camouflage

Organizations are optimized to reward silence.

Silence:

- Avoids conflict

- Preserves hierarchy

- Keeps meetings efficient

But silence is also the most reliable indicator of injury.

When high performers go silent, it means:

- Feedback is no longer safe

- Participation no longer feels reciprocal

- Identity is at risk

This is the point of no return most organizations miss.

---

10. Why Leaders Misdiagnose Disengagement

Leaders often misdiagnose disengagement as:

- Burnout

- Work-life imbalance

- Personal issues

These may be present.

But disengagement following public correction or recognition failure is not exhaustion.

It is **self-preservation**.

People disengage not because they are tired—but because participation has become unsafe to identity.

---

11. Metrics Hide Moral Damage

Organizations rely on metrics.

Metrics track:

- Output

- Revenue

- Efficiency

They do not track:

- Moral injury

- Status degradation

- Silent withdrawal

This is why leaders are surprised by sudden departures, cultural collapse, or performance cliffs.

The damage was never invisible.

It was just **unmeasured**.

---

12. Why This Framework Does Not Offer Solutions

At this point, readers often expect remedies.

They want:

- Recognition systems

- Feedback protocols

- Leadership training

This framework refuses to provide them.

Because the problem is not lack of technique.

It is **misplaced authority**.

Leaders know public humiliation is dangerous.
They know recognition matters.
They know silence is risky.

They do these things anyway—because hierarchy rewards short-term control over long-term alignment.

No checklist fixes that.

---

13. Application Without Repair: The Core Warning

This framework can be applied diagnostically in organizations to identify:

- Why top talent disengages

- Why performance persists before collapse

- Why culture rots quietly

- Why leaders are blindsided

What it cannot do is force repair.

Repair requires:

- Visible concession

- Status recalibration

- Public acknowledgment of harm

Most organizations will not do this.

Not because they are evil.
But because **authority resists visible loss**.

This is the tragedy.

---

14. The Organizational Iliad Repeats Daily

Every organization has its Achilles moments:

- A top performer publicly corrected

- A contribution erased

- A warning ignored

And every time, leadership believes:

> "They'll get over it."

They rarely do.

They adapt.
They disengage.
They leave.

The organization continues.

Until it doesn't.

---

15. Strategic Implication (Without Prescription)

This framework does not tell leaders what to do.

It tells them what is already happening.

If performance persists without recognition, then:

- Stability is illusory

- Silence is dangerous

- High output does not equal commitment

- Authority is masking decay

Ignoring these truths does not preserve organizations.

It delays collapse.

Closing Position

The Iliad is not a warning about ancient kings.

It is a mirror.

Achilles does not leave because he hates the Greeks.
 He leaves because the system no longer recognizes him safely.

Modern organizations lose their best people the same way.

Quietly.
 Rationally.
Without drama.

This chapter ends with the final truth of Part V:

> **Organizations do not fail because leaders lack
> solutions.**
> **They fail because leaders apply authority where
> dignity was required.**

And once dignity is lost,
 no framework—no matter how accurate—
 can restore what the system refused to protect.

Chapter 19

Political and Institutional Coalitions

Core Realities

**Factional pride hardens positions.
Status competition displaces governance.
Legitimacy collapses through disrespect—long before power
is lost.**

---

1. Why Political Coalitions Fail Differently—and the Same

Political and institutional coalitions appear durable.

They possess:

- Constitutions

- Procedures

- Offices

- Continuity beyond individuals

This creates the illusion that they fail **slowly**.

In reality, they fail **quietly**, then suddenly.

The Iliad demonstrates the template with brutal clarity:
formal authority persists; legitimacy evaporates.

This chapter establishes the AWH position:

> **Political coalitions rarely fall because enemies overwhelm them.**
> **They fall because internal respect collapses faster than rules can compensate.**

Institutions survive on paper long after belief withdraws.

---

2. Factional Pride: The Seed of Internal War

Factional pride is not ideology.

It is **identity defense** at scale.

Factions are not formed merely by policy preference.
They form around:

- Status recognition

- Historical grievance

- Symbolic hierarchy

- Perceived humiliation

Once factional pride hardens, compromise becomes **identity loss**.

In *The Iliad*, the Greek coalition is not ideologically divided.
It is **status-divided**.

Agamemnon and Achilles represent competing centers of pride.
Neither can yield publicly without injury.

This is the structural danger of factional pride:

> **When pride anchors identity, negotiation becomes existential.**

---

3. Why Factions Escalate Even When Objectives Align

Political coalitions often fracture even when they agree on goals.

Why?

Because agreement on outcomes does not resolve **competition over recognition**.

In *The Iliad*:

- Both sides want Troy defeated

- Both want Greek supremacy

- Both depend on each other

And yet, the coalition nearly collapses.

Because victory is not the only currency.

Status is.

This is the AWH diagnostic:

> **Coalitions fail when factions compete over who embodies legitimacy, not what must be done.**

---

4. Status Competition Displaces Governance

Once status competition dominates, governance degrades.

Decision-making shifts from:

- What works
   to

- Who wins

Policy becomes theater.
Process becomes signaling.
Compromise becomes weakness.

Agamemnon's actions are not strategic.
They are symbolic.

They demonstrate dominance.

This is how status competition hijacks institutions:

- Authority becomes performative

- Decisions prioritize visibility

- Outcomes become secondary

The institution still functions procedurally.
It no longer governs meaningfully.

---

5. Legitimacy vs. Authority in Political Systems

Political systems survive on legitimacy more than authority.

Authority enforces.
Legitimacy persuades.

When legitimacy erodes, authority grows louder.

This is not strength.
It is compensation.

In *The Iliad*, Agamemnon's authority remains unquestioned.
His legitimacy evaporates.

The coalition obeys.
It no longer believes.

This produces a familiar political pathology:

> **Institutions that rely increasingly on enforcement
> are already hollow.**

---

6. Disrespect as a Legitimacy-Killing Act

Disrespect in political systems is not rude behavior.

It is **a delegitimizing event**.

Public disrespect:

- Lowers status

- Signals exclusion

- Redefines hierarchy

When disrespect is tolerated or rewarded, legitimacy collapses
rapidly.

Achilles is not merely offended.
 He is **publicly reduced**.

That reduction signals to others:

- Excellence is unsafe

- Authority is arbitrary

- Participation is conditional

This is how disrespect kills coalitions without firing a shot.

---

7. Why Disrespect Spreads Faster Than Policy Failure

Policy failure can be debated.
 Disrespect cannot.

Once disrespect occurs:

- Witnesses update their expectations

- Factions entrench

- Trust collapses

Disrespect requires no interpretation.

It is seen.
It is remembered.
It is cumulative.

This is why political coalitions often survive disastrous policy—but collapse after symbolic insults.

---

8. The Audience Effect in Institutional Settings

Political actions are always performed before an audience:

- Constituents

- Bureaucrats

- Media

- Rival factions

Public disrespect has **second-order effects**:

- It licenses imitation

- It normalizes contempt

- It invites retaliation

In *The Iliad*, Achilles' humiliation is witnessed by the entire Greek assembly.

The damage is not contained between two men.
It becomes institutional knowledge.

---

9. Why Apologies Rarely Restore Legitimacy

Political systems often attempt repair through apology.

This almost always fails.

Why?

Because legitimacy loss is structural, not emotional.

Apologies that do not:

- Recalibrate status

- Acknowledge public harm publicly

- Impose cost on authority

are interpreted as tactical, not sincere.

Agamemnon's late concessions fail because they preserve hierarchy.

The injury stands.

This is the AWH rule:

> **Legitimacy lost through public disrespect cannot be restored privately or cheaply.**

---

10. Factional Silence as Institutional Decay

As legitimacy erodes, factions go silent.

Not inactive—silent.

They:

- Obstruct quietly

- Delay implementation

- Withdraw initiative

- Narrow cooperation

The institution still meets.
Votes still occur.
Processes still run.

But belief has left.

This is why political collapse surprises observers.

They were watching laws.
They missed alignment.

---

11. Status Competition Produces Governance Paralysis

When factions compete for status, every action becomes symbolic.

Even neutral decisions are interpreted as:

- Power grabs

- Insults

- Capitulations

This paralyzes governance.

No move is safe.
Every concession is betrayal.

The institution becomes trapped.

This is visible in *The Iliad*:

- Agamemnon cannot retreat

- Achilles cannot return

- The coalition bleeds

No one chooses collapse.
They become unable to prevent it.

---

12. Why Institutions Punish Dissent Instead of Disrespect

Institutions often punish dissent while ignoring disrespect.

Why?

Because dissent threatens outcomes.
Disrespect threatens authority.

Authority protects itself first.

This inversion accelerates legitimacy collapse.

Punishing dissent signals:

- Authority matters more than fairness

- Power outranks contribution

- Silence is safer than truth

This produces disengagement at scale.

---

13. Modern Political Coalitions, Same Pattern

The pattern persists across eras and systems:

- Legislatures paralyzed by factional pride

- Parties collapsing after symbolic disrespect

- Alliances breaking over status disputes

- Institutions surviving procedurally while losing belief

The names change.
 The structure does not.

The Iliad is not ancient history here.

It is template.

14. Why This Framework Does Not Offer Political Solutions

Readers often want reform here.

They want:

- Bipartisanship strategies

- Institutional redesign

- Norm restoration

This framework refuses.

Because political coalitions do not fail from lack of ideas.

They fail because:

- Pride overrides restraint

- Status competition overrides governance

- Authority resists visible concession

No technical fix solves that.

15. Strategic Implication (Without Prescription)

This framework diagnoses, it does not repair.

If political coalitions collapse through disrespect and status competition, then:

- Procedural strength cannot substitute for legitimacy

- Shared goals cannot overcome symbolic injury

- Silence must be treated as decay, not stability

- Authority preserved at the cost of respect is temporary

Ignoring these truths does not preserve institutions.

It accelerates their hollowing.

Closing Position

The Iliad does not depict the fall of Troy as the greatest tragedy.

It depicts the near-collapse of the Greek coalition—
not from defeat,
but from **internal disrespect**.

Political and institutional coalitions fail the same way.

Not when laws break.
 Not when enemies advance.

But when factions decide—quietly, irrevocably—
 that the institution no longer recognizes them with dignity.

This chapter leaves behind the final truth of political collapse:

**Power can persist without legitimacy.
 Institutions cannot.**

And once legitimacy is gone,
 no election, reform, or victory
 can restore what disrespect destroyed.

Chapter 20

Crisis, Loss, and Aftermath

Core Realities

Trauma reshapes leadership behavior.
Grief overrides procedural logic.
Systems fail quietly after visible success.

---

1. The Most Dangerous Phase Is After the Crisis

Most systems prepare for crisis.

They rehearse:

- Emergency protocols

- Escalation chains

- Decision rights

- Command authority

They assume that once the crisis passes, normal order resumes.

This assumption is false.

The most dangerous phase is **after** the crisis—
 when losses have been absorbed, victory declared, and leaders
are expected to "return to normal."

The Iliad makes this unmistakable.

The war does not end when Troy weakens.
 The coalition does not stabilize when Achilles returns.
 The greatest damage occurs **after** decisive moments—when
trauma and grief begin shaping behavior unchecked.

This chapter establishes the AWH position:

> **Crisis reveals systems.**
> **Aftermath destroys them.**

---

2. Trauma Does Not End When Events End

Trauma is not the event.

It is the **internal reorganization that follows exposure**.

In leadership contexts, trauma manifests as:

- Hyper-control

- Emotional volatility

- Narrowed tolerance for dissent

- Urgency detached from context

These are not character flaws.

They are adaptive responses carried forward into environments where they no longer fit.

Achilles does not stop being effective after Patroclus' death.
He becomes *more* effective—temporarily.

But his internal state has changed permanently.

The war's logic has not changed.
His behavior has.

This is the first failure mode of aftermath:

> **Leaders survive crises, but they do not exit them unchanged.**

3. How Trauma Reshapes Leadership Behavior

Trauma reshapes leaders along predictable lines:

1. **Control Increases** – Uncertainty becomes intolerable

2. **Time Horizons Collapse** – Long-term thinking gives way to immediacy

3. **Tolerance Shrinks** – Dissent feels like threat

4. **Procedure Feels Obstructive** – Rules slow emotional resolution

In *The Iliad*, Achilles' post-trauma behavior reflects all four.

He no longer negotiates.
He no longer delays.
He no longer accepts ritual constraint.

> *"Now I have no care for life, let it perish."*

This is not despair.
It is **trauma-driven reprioritization**.

Leadership behavior adapts to internal injury—not external reality.

4. Grief Overrides Procedural Logic

Procedures exist to:

- Slow decision-making

- Enforce proportionality

- Preserve predictability

Grief makes these feel irrelevant.

When leaders grieve:

- Process feels disrespectful

- Delay feels cruel

- Boundaries feel arbitrary

Achilles does not violate procedure because he is undisciplined.
He violates it because grief has rewritten what matters.

Dragging Hector's body is not tactical.
It is expressive.

This is the AWH diagnostic:

> **Grief converts systems designed for outcomes
> into instruments for emotional discharge.**

Once this happens, procedure loses authority—even if it remains formally intact.

---

5. Why Procedure Cannot Compete with Loss

Procedures assume shared future orientation.

Grief collapses the future into the present.

When leaders are grieving:

- Long-term consequences lose weight

- Institutional memory fades

- Symbolic acts dominate

This is why post-crisis governance so often fails.

Not because leaders are incompetent—
but because their **internal state no longer aligns with the system's design assumptions**.

Procedure cannot override grief.
It can only be ignored by it.

---

6. The Illusion of Stability After Victory

Victory creates a false signal.

When outcomes improve:

- Leaders believe the system is healing

- Observers believe the danger has passed

- Institutions declare success

In *The Iliad*, Achilles' return shifts the war decisively.

From the outside:

- The Greeks are winning

- The crisis appears resolved

Internally:

- Trauma is active

- Moral injury is accumulating

- Restraint has collapsed

This creates the most dangerous illusion in systems:

Visible success masks internal failure.

---

7. Systems Fail Quietly After Visible Success

Systems rarely collapse at their weakest moment.

They collapse when:

- Exhaustion sets in

- Trauma goes unaddressed

- Alignment is assumed restored

This is why post-crisis periods are lethal.

People expect relief.
 They receive continued pressure.
 They disengage silently.

In *The Iliad*, the war's end does not restore wholeness.
 It leaves survivors carrying unintegrated loss.

The coalition holds—until it doesn't.

---

8. Trauma Propagates Downward

Leader trauma does not remain isolated.

It spreads through:

- Tone

- Decision velocity

- Punitive reflexes

- Loss of patience

Subordinates adapt.

They become cautious.
They become silent.
They stop offering dissent.

This is not loyalty.
It is **self-protection**.

The system becomes brittle—less capable of absorbing new stress.

9. Why Leaders Misinterpret Post-Crisis Behavior

After crises, leaders often misread signals.

They see:

- Reduced dissent → agreement

- Faster execution → alignment

- Silence → relief

They are wrong.

These are symptoms of:

- Trauma-driven compliance

- Emotional withdrawal

- Exhaustion

The AWH warning here is precise:

> **Post-crisis quiet is not recovery.
> It is often injury consolidating.**

10. The Collapse of Learning After Crisis

Healthy systems learn from crisis.

Traumatized systems avoid reflection.

Why?

Because reflection requires revisiting loss.
 And grief resists reopening wounds.

In *The Iliad*, there is no debrief.
 No integration.
 No reckoning.

The war ends.
 The cost remains.

This is why systems repeat failure patterns.

Not because they forgot.
 Because they **could not tolerate remembering**.

---

11. Aftermath and the Rewriting of Identity

Trauma reshapes identity.

Leaders who survive crisis often:

- Define themselves by endurance

- Mistake survival for correctness

- Equate control with safety

This identity hardens.

It resists correction.
 It rejects vulnerability.
 It demands compliance.

Over time, this alienates the very coalition that enabled survival.

---

12. Why Repair Rarely Occurs After Crisis

Repair requires:

- Slowing down

- Naming loss

- Acknowledging harm

- Accepting diminished authority

Most leaders cannot do this immediately after crisis.

They are depleted.
 They are reactive.
 They are praised for survival.

This makes repair structurally unlikely.

The system moves on.
 The injury stays.

---

13. Modern Systems, Same Pattern

This failure mode is everywhere:

- Organizations that "win" restructuring but lose talent

- Governments that survive emergencies but fracture afterward

- Militaries that prevail tactically and suffer long-term collapse

- Movements that succeed publicly and dissolve privately

In every case:

- Crisis performance is celebrated

- Aftermath damage is ignored

Until it surfaces years later.

---

14. Why This Framework Still Does Not Offer Repair

At this point, readers often demand solutions.

They ask:

- How do leaders heal?

- How do systems recover?

- How do coalitions reintegrate after loss?

This framework does not answer.

Not because repair is impossible—
but because **most systems will not pay the cost of repair**.

Repair requires:

- Visible humility

- Status recalibration

- Public acknowledgment of harm

Authority resists all three.

So the framework remains diagnostic.

---

15. Strategic Implication (Without Prescription)

This framework does not teach crisis leadership.
It teaches **post-crisis recognition**.

If trauma reshapes leadership and grief overrides procedure, then:

- Success cannot be treated as stability

- Quiet must be treated as risk

- Control must be treated with suspicion

- Aftermath must be considered a separate danger phase

Ignoring these truths does not preserve systems.

It delays their collapse.

Closing Position

The Iliad does not end with peace.

It ends with mourning.

Priam retrieves Hector's body.
 Achilles pauses—not healed, not restored, but momentarily
human again.

The war is effectively over.
 The cost remains.

This chapter closes the framework with its final, hardest truth:

> **Systems do not fail at the height of crisis.**
> **They fail in the aftermath—when loss has**
> **changed leaders,**
> **and no one recalibrates for what that change**
> **means.**

Victory does not reset the system.
 Survival does not restore alignment.
 Procedure does not override grief.

And when leaders carry trauma forward unexamined,
 the system will appear to function—
 until one day, quietly,
 it no longer does.

PART VI

RELATION TO OTHER FRAMEWORKS

Why This Framework Is Necessary but Insufficient Alone

Chapter 21

Why *The Art of War* Is Insufficient

Core Realities

Correct decisions can still destroy morale.
Cost models ignore emotional injury.
Restraint does not heal humiliation.

---

1. The Problem Is Not That *The Art of War* Is Wrong

This framework does not argue against *The Art of War*.

It depends on it.

Sun Tzu's work remains one of the most accurate decision engines ever written:

- It prioritizes efficiency

- It minimizes unnecessary cost

- It favors restraint, preparation, and indirect action

- It treats war as a problem of timing, terrain, and deception

These insights remain correct.

And yet, when applied alone, *The Art of War* fails catastrophically in environments where **human injury** dominates system behavior.

This chapter establishes the AWH position clearly:

> **The Art of War optimizes decisions.**
> **It does not diagnose human fracture.**

That gap is not theoretical.
It is lethal.

---

2. Optimization Is Not the Same as Preservation

The Art of War assumes a stable decision-maker.

Its logic presumes:

- Actors respond predictably to incentives

- Losses are assessed rationally

- Morale can be managed through structure and discipline

- Victory clarifies legitimacy

These assumptions hold in **mechanical systems**.

They fail in **human systems under injury**.

In *The Iliad*, many of Agamemnon's decisions are strategically defensible.
 They are also coalition-destroying.

This is the first contradiction this chapter isolates:

> **A decision can be strategically correct
> and still be systemically fatal.**

Sun Tzu tells you how to win.
 He does not tell you what winning does to wounded people.

3. Correct Decisions Can Still Destroy Morale

From a Sun Tzu perspective, Agamemnon's actions can be defended:

- Authority must be preserved

- Challenges to command cannot be allowed publicly

- Discipline requires visible enforcement

These are rational assertions.

They are also disastrous.

Because morale is not preserved by correctness.
It is preserved by **recognition, dignity, and proportionality**.

The Iliad demonstrates that morale collapses not when decisions are wrong—but when **people feel erased by them**.

This is the AWH correction:

> **Morale is not a variable you optimize.**
> **It is a condition you preserve—or**
> **destroy—through treatment.**

4. Why Cost Models Fail in Human Systems

The Art of War is fundamentally a cost-minimization framework.

It tracks:

- Troop loss

- Resource expenditure

- Time

- Exposure

What it does not track:

- Humiliation

- Moral injury

- Status degradation

- Identity fracture

These costs are not visible on ledgers.
They do not appear in after-action reports.
They do not register until it is too late.

In *The Iliad*, the Greeks pay little immediate cost for humiliating Achilles.

The true cost arrives later:

- Withdrawal

- Escalation

- Catastrophic losses

This exposes the second insufficiency:

**Cost models that ignore emotional injury
systematically underestimate future collapse.**

Sun Tzu teaches you to count bodies and supplies.
Homer shows you what happens when you ignore the human ledger.

---

5. The Art of War Assumes Substitutability

One of Sun Tzu's implicit assumptions is substitutability.

Generals are interchangeable.
Units can be redeployed.
Losses can be compensated.

This assumption holds at scale.

It fails at the **symbolic level**.

Achilles is not substitutable.

Not because of skill alone—but because of meaning.

His withdrawal removes:

- Combat power

- Symbolic center

- Identity anchor

The Art of War recognizes the value of exceptional generals. It does not account for **what happens when exceptional contributors are injured rather than defeated**.

This is a different failure mode.

---

6. Restraint Does Not Heal Humiliation

Sun Tzu prizes restraint:

- Avoid unnecessary battle

- Control emotion

- Preserve force

These are correct prescriptions.

But restraint is **preventative**, not curative.

Once humiliation occurs, restraint alone cannot repair it.

Agamemnon's later restraint—offers of gifts, delayed concessions—fails completely.

Why?

Because humiliation is a **public structural injury**, not an emotional spike.

This yields the third core insight of this chapter:

> **Restraint prevents damage.**
> **It does not reverse it.**

The Art of War teaches how to avoid unnecessary conflict. It does not teach how to reconstitute legitimacy after it is shattered.

---

7. Decision Discipline vs. Human Memory

Sun Tzu's framework assumes decisions are discrete.

Make the right move.
 Advance.
 Win.
 Proceed.

Human systems do not work that way.

Humans carry memory.
 Memory accumulates.
 Memory compounds.

In *The Iliad*, Achilles does not reset after Agamemnon's later apologies.

The injury has already rewritten identity.

This is where decision theory fails:

> **Humans do not reset between moves.**
> **They carry the previous move forward into every future one.**

No optimization framework can override that.

---

8. Why Art of War Practitioners Are Often Blindsided

Leaders trained primarily in Sun Tzu are often shocked by collapse.

They say:

- "The decision was sound."

- "The incentives were aligned."

- "The cost-benefit analysis was clear."

All true.

All irrelevant.

Because the failure occurred **below the level of rational calculation**.

It occurred in dignity, pride, honor, and injury.

Sun Tzu does not deny these forces.
He simply does not model them.

---

9. The Iliad Explains What Sun Tzu Assumes Away

This is not a contradiction between frameworks.

It is a division of labor.

- *The Art of War* explains **how to decide under conflict**

- *The Iliad* reveals **why systems still collapse afterward**

Sun Tzu teaches control.
Homer teaches consequence.

One without the other produces leaders who are:

- Tactically brilliant

- Systemically blind

This framework exists to close that gap.

---

10. Emotional Injury as a Strategic Force

Sun Tzu treats emotion as something to be controlled.

The Iliad treats emotion as something that **acts back on the system**.

Rage escalates conflict.
Grief rewrites objectives.
Humiliation fractures coalitions.

These are not distractions from strategy.
They are **strategic forces**.

Ignoring them does not make them disappear.
It hands them control.

---

11. Why Winning Makes This Worse

One of the most dangerous misunderstandings in Sun Tzu–only thinking is this:

Victory resolves problems.

In human systems, victory often **conceals** them.

After victory:

- Loss is unacknowledged

- Injury is minimized

- Silence is misread as closure

The Iliad ends not with triumph—but with mourning.

Because the true damage appears **after** success.

This is where *The Art of War* falls silent.

---

12. This Framework Does Not Replace Sun Tzu

This chapter does not propose abandoning *The Art of War*.

That would be foolish.

Sun Tzu remains essential for:

- Pre-action discipline

- Strategic clarity

- Cost containment

- Timing and positioning

But it must be paired with a failure-diagnostic lens.

The AWH position is precise:

> **Use The Art of War to decide.**
> **Use The Iliad to understand what your decisions do to people.**

One without the other produces collapse with efficiency.

---

13. Why This Framework Still Does Not "Fix" the Problem

Even with both frameworks, collapse often persists.

Why?

Because recognizing injury does not obligate systems to repair it.

Repair requires:

- Visible concession

- Status recalibration

- Acceptance of authority loss

Most leaders will not pay that price.

So the framework remains diagnostic.

It tells you:

- Why morale collapsed despite correct decisions

- Why restraint failed to restore unity

- Why cost models underestimated damage

It does not promise recovery.

14. The Cost of Ignoring This Limitation

Leaders who rely solely on Sun Tzu:

- Optimize their way into disengagement

- Control their way into silence

- Win battles and lose coalitions

This is not theoretical.
 It is observable across:

- Militaries

- Corporations

- Political institutions

- Movements

The pattern repeats because the injury is invisible to the model.

15. Strategic Implication (Without Prescription)

This framework does not replace *The Art of War*.
It bounds it.

If *The Art of War* is insufficient alone, then:

- Correctness must not be confused with sustainability

- Cost models must be treated as incomplete

- Restraint must be understood as preventative, not reparative

- Victory must be treated as a risk phase, not a resolution

Ignoring these truths does not make leaders more decisive.

It makes them more dangerous.

Closing Position

The Art of War teaches how to win without fighting.

The Iliad shows what happens when winning still breaks the system.

This chapter leaves behind the essential conclusion of Part VI:

**A framework that optimizes decisions but ignores injury
 will produce victories that destroy what they were meant to preserve.**

Sun Tzu tells you how not to lose the war.

Homer tells you why, even then,
 you may still lose everything that mattered.

Chapter 22

Why *The Prince* Is Insufficient

Core Realities

**Power can persist while coalitions rot.
Authority cannot command loyalty.
Legitimacy does not repair pride.**

---

1. The Problem Is Not That Machiavelli Is Cynical

Machiavelli is not wrong.

The Prince remains one of the clearest-eyed analyses of power ever written. It strips away moral fantasy and addresses politics as it is practiced, not as it is preached. It explains:

- How rulers acquire power

- How rulers retain power

- How fear, reward, and perception shape obedience

- How instability is managed through decisive action

These insights are accurate.

They are also incomplete.

This framework does not challenge Machiavelli's realism.
It challenges his **assumptions about what power preserves**.

The AWH position is precise:

> **Machiavelli explains how rulers survive.**
> **He does not explain how systems remain intact**
> **around them.**

That difference is everything.

---

2. Power Survival vs. System Survival

Machiavelli optimizes for ruler survival.

His unit of analysis is the prince—not the coalition, not the institution, not the long-term social fabric.

From that perspective:

- Fear is effective

- Force is efficient

- Legitimacy is useful but optional

- Love is unreliable

And often, he is correct.

But *The Iliad* shows something Machiavelli does not model:

> **A ruler can survive while the system around him disintegrates.**

Agamemnon never loses his crown.
He never loses formal authority.
He never loses command.

Yet the coalition nearly collapses.

Power persists.
Alignment dies.

This distinction is where Machiavelli stops—and where this framework begins.

---

3. Power Can Persist While Coalitions Rot

One of the most dangerous illusions in leadership is equating endurance with health.

Machiavellian logic reinforces this illusion.

If:

- The ruler remains in control

- Orders are followed

- Structures remain intact

Then power appears stable.

In *The Iliad*, this illusion holds for most of the war.

Agamemnon commands.
The army fights.
The hierarchy functions.

And yet:

- Trust erodes

- Loyalty thins

- Silence spreads

- Withdrawal occurs

This reveals a core AWH insight:

Power persistence is not evidence of coalition integrity.

Machiavelli teaches leaders to survive collapse conditions. He does not teach them to recognize collapse **before** survival becomes the only objective.

---

4. Authority Can Compel Action, Not Belief

Machiavelli understands this implicitly.

He never claims authority produces loyalty. He claims it produces obedience.

The problem is not Machiavelli's claim.

The problem is what leaders assume beyond it.

Many leaders believe:

- Authority should produce loyalty

- Compliance implies belief

- Fear stabilizes systems

The Iliad disproves all three.

Greek warriors obey.
They fight.
They die.

They do not believe.

Achilles withdraws not because he lacks fear—but because authority has become **identity-threatening**.

This produces the second core insight of this chapter:

> **Authority can command action.**
> **It cannot command loyalty.**

And systems that confuse the two rot quietly.

---

5. Fear Is Effective—and Corrosive

Machiavelli famously argues it is safer to be feared than loved.

This is often misinterpreted as endorsement of cruelty.

It is not.

It is an observation about predictability.

Fear produces compliance.

What Machiavelli does not model is **what fear does over time inside coalitions**.

Fear:

- Narrows initiative
- Silences feedback
- Encourages withdrawal
- Concentrates decision-making

These effects do not destabilize the ruler immediately.

They destabilize the **system's adaptive capacity**.

In *The Iliad*, fear keeps soldiers fighting.
It does not keep them aligned.

This is why Machiavellian systems often survive crises—but fail afterward.

---

6. Legitimacy Is Instrumental in Machiavelli, Existential in Homer

Machiavelli treats legitimacy as instrumental.

It is useful when available.
Replaceable when not.

Homer treats legitimacy as **existential**.

Once legitimacy collapses, participation becomes psychologically impossible for key actors.

Achilles does not debate legitimacy.
He experiences its loss as annihilation.

This is the third core insight of this chapter:

> **Legitimacy can maintain obedience.**
> **It cannot repair injured pride.**

Once pride is injured publicly, legitimacy becomes irrelevant to the injured party.

Machiavelli does not account for this boundary condition.

---

7. Pride Injury Is Not a Power Problem

Pride injury is not solved by:

- Threats

- Rewards

- Legitimacy signals

- Institutional continuity

Because pride is not about authority.

It is about **self-recognition**.

Agamemnon's later attempts to repair the rupture fail not because they are insufficient—but because they arrive **after identity fracture**.

From a Machiavellian view:

- Gifts should work

- Apology should suffice

- Authority remains intact

From a human view:

- The injury is irreversible

This is why legitimacy does not repair pride once publicly broken.

---

8. Machiavelli Assumes Replaceability Where It Does Not Exist

Machiavellian power assumes actors are replaceable.

If one ally withdraws, others fill the gap.
If one noble resists, others comply.

This assumption holds in many political contexts.

It fails when **symbolic actors** are injured.

Achilles is not just a warrior.
He is the coalition's meaning center.

His withdrawal removes something no substitute can restore.

Machiavelli recognizes exceptional individuals.
He does not model **exceptional injury**.

---

9. Silence Breaks Machiavellian Detection

Machiavelli expects resistance to manifest visibly.

Plots.
Revolts.
Conspiracies.

He advises princes how to detect and crush them.

What he does not address is **silent withdrawal**.

Silence produces no conspiracy.
No plot.
No rebellion.

And yet it drains systems faster than open resistance.

Achilles does not conspire.
 He goes quiet.

The system bleeds anyway.

This is where Machiavelli's toolkit fails.

---

10. Why Leaders Misapply Machiavelli to Coalitions

Leaders often use Machiavellian logic to manage coalitions.

They believe:

- Fear will keep factions in line

- Authority will suppress dissent

- Power projection will restore unity

These tactics preserve control.

They destroy cohesion.

The result is a ruler who survives—
 presiding over an increasingly hollow system.

---

11. The Prince Explains Survival, Not Meaning

Machiavelli never claims to preserve meaning.

He assumes rulers care about power.

But most leaders want more than survival.

They want:

- Loyalty

- Alignment

- Legacy

- Functional systems

Machiavellian logic undermines these aims over time.

Not immediately.
 Predictably.

This is the structural mismatch.

12. Why Power Alone Cannot Prevent Collapse

Power prevents overthrow.
 It does not prevent disengagement.

In *The Iliad*:

- No one overthrows Agamemnon

- No coup occurs

- Authority stands

And yet the coalition nearly fails.

This exposes the fatal limitation:

> **Power protects the ruler.**
> **It does not protect the system.**

---

13. Modern Systems Repeat This Error Constantly

The pattern is everywhere:

- CEOs retain control while companies hollow out

- Political leaders remain in office while institutions decay

- Regimes persist while legitimacy collapses

Observers ask:

"How did this fall apart so suddenly?"

It didn't.

Power masked the rot.

---

14. Why This Framework Still Does Not Replace Machiavelli

This chapter does not discard Machiavelli.

That would be naïve.

Power must still be understood.
Authority must still be managed.
Fear remains a real force.

The AWH position is additive, not oppositional:

Use Machiavelli to understand how power survives.
Use Homer to understand why systems still fail around it.

One explains endurance.
 The other explains collapse.

---

15. Strategic Implication (Without Prescription)

This framework does not offer an alternative power doctrine.

It diagnoses a limit.

If *The Prince* is insufficient alone, then:

- Power persistence must not be mistaken for system health

- Authority must not be assumed to generate loyalty

- Legitimacy must not be assumed to repair pride

- Silence must not be interpreted as stability

Ignoring these truths produces rulers who survive—
leading systems that do not.

Closing Position

Machiavelli teaches leaders how to remain standing.

Homer shows what remains standing **after** everyone else has disengaged.

Agamemnon keeps his crown.
 Achilles withdraws.
 The coalition bleeds.

This chapter closes Part VI with its final truth:

> **Power can endure without loyalty.**
> **Authority can function without belief.**
> **And legitimacy, once pride is broken, cannot put the system back together.**

That is why *The Prince* is necessary.

And why, by itself,
 it is never enough.

Before You Close This Book

You did not just read a leadership book.
You did not read a strategy guide.
You did not read a story about heroes, growth, or resolution.

You read a **failure-diagnostic framework**.

This book was not written to help you *lead better*.
It was written to help you **see collapse earlier**—
before it announces itself,
before it becomes public,
before it is irreversible.

What This Book Actually Gave You

Most frameworks teach you how to act.

This one taught you **what breaks**.

You now understand:

- Why correct decisions can still destroy morale

- Why authority persists while coalitions rot

- Why silence is more dangerous than dissent

- Why humiliation cannot be undone by apology

- Why grief overrides procedure

- Why victory often conceals damage instead of resolving it

You were not shown how to win.

You were shown **why winning sometimes destroys the system that achieved it**.

Why This Framework Is Uncomfortable

Because it removes excuses.

After this book, you can no longer rely on:

- "The numbers supported it"

- "The strategy was sound"

- "They should understand"

- "We were still performing"

This framework exposes a harder truth:

Systems don't fail when leaders are wrong.
 They fail when leaders are **right—and blind to human cost**.

That is not a comforting insight.
 It is a necessary one.

What This Book Does *Not* Promise

It does not promise:

- Harmony

- Healing

- Loyalty

- Reconciliation

- Cultural transformation

Those outcomes require conditions most systems refuse to meet.

This book does not pretend otherwise.

It gives you something more honest:

Early visibility into failure while it is still quiet.

Who This Book Is For

This framework is for people who operate inside systems where:

- Power is intact, but trust is thinning

- Performance is high, but belief is fading

- Silence feels like relief—but isn't

- Authority still works—but alignment doesn't

If you lead, advise, govern, command, negotiate, or build coalitions—
 this book was written for the moments **before** things break publicly.

What Comes After This Page

Nothing actionable.
 No checklist.
 No call to "be better."

That is intentional.

The moment you try to *use* this framework to fix people, it stops working.

Its role is narrower—and more dangerous:

To tell you when you are standing on a fault line
even though the structure still looks intact.

What you do with that knowledge is your responsibility.

Final Reminder

The Iliad does not end in triumph.
 It ends in mourning.

Not because the war was lost—
 but because something essential didn't survive victory.

This framework exists so that, next time,
 you recognize that moment **before** it arrives disguised as
success.

Close the book when you're ready.

Just don't forget what it showed you.

THIS IS NOT A COLLECTION

This volume is part of **Ancient Wisdom Hacks**—
an ongoing body of work focused on how strategy, power, and
failure actually function under pressure.

The books are only one layer.

What you are reading is an entry point into a larger system of
interpretation, application, and expansion.

WHAT THESE WORKS ARE DESIGNED TO DO

Most people look for answers.

These works expose patterns:

- How decisions are made before they are visible
- How systems weaken before they collapse
- How power shifts before it is recognized

This is not theory.
It is applied observation.

THE SYSTEM BEHIND THE WORK

Across all volumes and future releases, three forces remain
constant:

- **Strategy** — how outcomes are shaped before action
- **Conflict** — how people and systems break under pressure
- **Power** — how control is gained, maintained, and lost

No single book contains the full picture.
Each adds another angle.

CONTINUE BEYOND THIS VOLUME

New interpretations, applied volumes, and extended works are released continuously.

To access current and future material, visit:

www.AncientWisdomHacks.com

WHAT YOU WILL FIND

- Additional applied volumes across industries
- Expanded interpretations of foundational texts
- New releases not available through standard distribution
- Future projects extending beyond books

The system is still expanding.

FINAL POSITION

Clarity does not make outcomes easier.

It removes the illusion that they were ever simple.

Ancient Wisdom Hacks
Interpretation over repetition.
Application over theory.